CW01457431

Witchcraft

A Strange Conflict

Witchcraft
A Strange Conflict

by

Peter Hough

THE LUTTERWORTH PRESS
CAMBRIDGE

The Lutterworth Press
P.O. Box 60
Cambridge CB1 2NT

Copyright © Peter Hough 1991

British Library Cataloguing-in-Publication Data:
Hough, Peter
  Witchcraft : a strange conflict.
  I. Title
  133.43

ISBN 0-7188-2809-7

All rights reserved. No part of this publication may be
reproduced, stored in a retrieval system or transmitted
in any way or by any means, mechanical, electronic,
photocopying or recording without the prior permission
in writing of the publisher.

Printed in Great Britain by
The Guernsey Press Co. Ltd, Guernsey, Channel Islands

For
Jenny Randles
Who in the beginning helped make the breaks happen

ACKNOWLEDGEMENTS

I would like to thank all those who allowed me interviews and sometimes suffered my impertinent questions. Many of them also provided me with invaluable documentation and the loan of books. I would like to say a big 'thank you'.

There were also others who in their own unique way helped me with pieces of the jigsaw. I would like to acknowledge the staff of Leigh Library (despite the fines), Shelley Bovey, gun slinger Robert Harvey (my spiritual guardian), John Haines, Rae Laurance, Mike Sacks, Geoffrey Simm, my mother, who looked out for cuttings for me, and my long-suffering family - particularly my wife, Valerie.

CONTENTS

INTRODUCTION

The reporter was too stunned to scoff. "You're talking about witchcraft, here, now, in the twentieth century?"

Delgard smiled weakly and finally tore his eyes away from the oak. "It's by no means unusual nowadays; there are many witches' covens throughout the British Isles. We laugh at such ideas today because it's comfortable for us to do so, and our scientific technology precludes such notions. This force must emanate from somewhere."

"What force is that?"

"The force of evil. Can't you feel it around us?"

This extract from the James Herbert novel, *Shrine*, sums up how many of us feel about the subject of witchcraft. Some people are surprised that witchcraft is practised at all today, and many believe that, in reality, it is just a handful of eccentrics indulging in a bit of harmless fun. Others deny it a supernatural element, believing witchcraft is merely a screen for fornication and sadism. The popular press pander to these scenarios by printing stories designed to liven up a wet Sunday morning, of nude orgies and the ritualistic sacrifice of family pets.

More seriously, a group of highly visible Christians have been linking child abuse - and even child sacrifice - with black witchcraft, or Satanism, both here and in the United States. Their campaign has succeeded in convincing many social workers of the reality of Satanic ritual abuse.

1

The witches I have spoken to deny these things go on. One said that she deters minors from becoming involved in something of which they have little understanding, and explained there are rigorous induction tests before candidates are allowed into covens. But as one modern witchfinder said to me: "They would say that wouldn't they?"

Another witch told me she was approached by what she called 'the Christian Mafia', who promised to 'leave her alone' in exchange for names and addresses of other practising witches and occultists. She, and many like her, say they are being victimised for practising paganism - a religion which, it is claimed, pre-dates Christianity by a thousand years. Modern paganism has as its head the Earth Mother, and allegedly utilises a natural 'magic' found in mountains, rivers and sacred groves. But according to Christian commentators, at the root of this religion with its fashionably 'Green' message, is Satan using it as a cover for more evil ambitions.

You will find in this book individuals offering first-hand knowledge of demonic activity. People like Colin Hale, a witch for eleven years, who experienced near fatal consequences while trying to break away from the Craft with the help of his Christian girlfriend. There were threatening telephone calls, the alleged materialisation of demonic entities and finally the phenomenon of possession - verified by the vicar who helped exorcise him.

There are stories of bloody sacrifice, diabolical curses, and arson in the wake of a national television programme on black magic.

On the other hand, there are accounts from Christians who have shed their faith for a pagan way of life. I have talked to Church of England ministers, Catholic priests, Christian help groups, witches and even a practising High Priest of Satanism.

Why did I decide to write this book?

For centuries a war has been going on. This has nothing to do with military adventurism or political terrorism. It is something more fundamental. Some people refer to it as the eternal war between good and evil, others say that it is a battle between the old religion and the new religion. Others still, claim it is a war against ignorance, prejudice and superstition. Whatever it is, it remains a conflict, and it is happening right this moment.

Since witchcraft came out of the closet in the 1950s its popularity has increased, causing one businessman who deals in mail order occult paraphernalia to boast that there are over 100,000 witches in Britain today. With this increase in interest, members of the Christian Church have become more vocal on the subject to counter-attack what they see as a threat to the very fabric of society.

In this dark tangled web of human, and perhaps, superhuman conflict, where lies the truth and where the fiction?

Now more than at any other time, the witchcraft debate is receiving a prolific public airing. Social workers and psychiatrists are claiming that young children are falling victim to organised networks of witch families and other occultists. Like thousands of other people I have followed the debate in newspapers, on the radio and on television. During this time, several things have struck me: There is a strong polarisation of opinion on the subject, and claims are often made which are contradicted by one side or another. On top of this some sections of the media tend to report events with a degree of bias, dependent on whether they see the subject as pure titillation, as a genuine spiritual threat to 'innocent' people, or as the perpetration of a new witch hunt.

I started asking myself lots of questions. What is witchcraft? Are witchcraft and Satanism really separate doctrines, as some claim? Is it just a case of a bunch of harmless eccentrics dressing up and having fun? Is it a cover for serious crime and the activities of sadists and paedophiles? Could it be an authentic religion ? Just how widespread is the cult? Can witches really work spells and conjure up supernatural agencies? Do Christians have a need to warn us to steer clear of occultism, or is it a case of 'sour grapes' because this alternative doctrine seems to be gaining ground at the expense of Christianity? Some Christians believe that Satan is a real demonic entity. Are they right to assume that Satan is hiding behind the veil of paganism? Is there any difference between 'white' witchcraft and 'black' witchcraft? Are babies really being butchered on Satanic altars?

This is the function of this book: finding out; looking to the past and seeing how it has affected the present; asking some fundamental questions of those who profess to know the answers; searching for evidence; allowing the pages of this book to be a forum for representatives of all complexions to voice their opinions - something which has not been done before.

Of course witchcraft is a world-wide phenomenon, particularly ingrained in native African culture. Whilst acknowledging this fact, the current work is concerned primarily with the conflict between Wicca - the term witches use to describe their craft - and Christian fundamentalism as it affects Western society.

Using my investigative and journalistic experience, fortified with objectivity - I have no axe to grind with either side - I hope I have helped to answer some of the questions many of you, like me, will have often asked.

Chapter One

OUT OF THE FIRE

The devil finds some mischief still for hands that have not learnt to be idle. Geoffrey Madan

"Most people don't realise it, but all around us there's a war being fought."

I was at the home of Merseyside couple Pamela and Colin Hale. Colin was not referring to military conflict. He was talking about the archaic war between good and evil, God and the Devil. And he should know, claiming to have fought and won that battle after eleven years in the grip of witchcraft. The Hales had agreed to tell me their story as a warning to others not to become embroiled in the occult, no matter how innocent it may seem on the surface.

Colin fixed me with a baleful stare. "A lot of what you're going to hear you won't believe. But it happened. All of it."

It was the mid-sixties, he was seventeen, and living in Somerset when it started. His seduction into witchcraft was both subtle and accidental.

"A group of us were discussing the occult one evening over a drink. It was one of those very hypothetical discussions like the meaning of life. Then someone said they knew of a group who met regularly to talk about this stuff, and would I like to go along? I just got involved. It was as easy and as simple as that.

5

"I wasn't particularly serious at first. I saw myself as a knight in shining armour - a white witch - ready to do battle with evil. Only much later did its true colours come out. We worshipped a hierarchy of deities. At the top were the Lords of Light, a group of Dr Who-type characters."

Colin was a design engineer for a company affiliated to British Aerospace. Several years later, the company moved him up to Manchester. There he met a girl and they got married, even though she knew nothing of his Wiccan practices. He joined one of four covens which were operating in the area at that time. Just how did he manage to keep his involvement from his first wife?

"I had to work a lot of 'overtime', travel away 'on business', and when I ran out of those excuses, I simply knocked her out with a sleeping draught. It wasn't all spells; we used a lot of natural chemicals. There are beneficial substances, harmful ones, and those in-between, which, for instance, can induce sleep... Take 'magic mushrooms', for instance. They've been around for thousands of years, but they've just been re-discovered as a substitute for glue."

But the undercurrents of Colin's double life did eventually lead to the breakdown of his marriage. At about the same time he went to work for another engineering company, this time based in St Helens. Pamela was already employed there as a receptionist.

"In the beginning there wasn't any real relationship, just a few jokes, a laugh, often at her expense. But all that was to change."

What brought about that change was a frightening dream experienced by Pamela. In the dream, she was standing in a graveyard situated not far from where she worked. Staring at one particular grave, the figure of Colin suddenly arose from it and stood beside her on the edge. As the dream faded, they both stared at the name and date engraved into the headstone. The dream played on her mind all the way to work the following morning.

"The Managing Director's secretary was a close friend of mine, and she agreed to visit the graveyard with me during lunch. Everything was there - exactly as I had dreamt it. That same day, I saw Colin and just blurted it out. I told him there was something very strange about him which frightened me, but he just smiled and left it at that. Then, sometime later, he took me out for a drink and told me the whole story."

They decided to do some research, and discovered that although the man had been buried in St Helens some two hundred years ago, he had lived all his life in Knowsley, working on Lord Derby's estate. Why wasn't he buried with his relatives in Knowsley? The couple learned that in the eighteenth century, anyone found practising witchcraft was denied burial in their own parish. Some old maps confirmed that St Helens formed the parish boundary with Knowsley in those days.

Was the dream a warning to Pamela that Colin was mixed up in occultism? Either way, Colin decided the man's spirit needed laying to rest, and consulted several ancient books for the correct 'formula'.

"That was one of the things which drew me towards witchcraft in the first place." He explained, " As an engineer, witchcraft formulas, or 'spells', seemed compatible with technical formulas. One carried out an action, and it had a specified reaction."

Pamela grudgingly agreed to help, and they drove up to Cumbria and visited an ancient row of standing stones called 'Old Meg'. Bits of the stone were chipped off for use in the ritual, but the ceremony fell apart.

"In the end, Pamela wouldn't go along with it. That was when the conflict really began. I was becoming very fond of her. There grew a division of loyalties. I was determined to get her in, and she was just as determined to get me out. The witchcraft hierarchy quickly drew ranks behind me. Once you're involved in witchcraft it's very hard to leave, in fact they don't like you even thinking of leaving."

"I was a Sunday School teacher," Pamela interjected, "I had always gone to church, and when I realised exactly what he was mixed up in, my prime intention was to get him out anyway I could. Initially, that was my only reason for seeing him."

Colin was now twenty-seven. Suddenly, in the midst of all this, he was promoted to High Priest. Colin feels this was too timely to be mere coincidence.

"That meant I could form a coven of my own. But to do that I needed a Priestess...all I had to do was persuade Pamela. That's how they work. They dangle a carrot before you, making you more determined."

But Pamela was unrelenting. She knew Colin's marriage was over, and that he was falling in love with her, and saw nothing wrong in using that emotional tie as a lever.

"I said you either quit, or I'll not even talk to you anymore. That was how desperate I was."

This ultimatum was a watershed for Colin.

"I was now head over heels in love with Pamela, and I didn't want to lose her. I started talking and thinking of getting out. It was then I began experiencing the power of auto-suggestion. I knew the coven was working spells against us, and things began to happen."

Pamela received death threats on the phone, delivered by a voice which she describes as 'weird' - neither male nor female, and ageless.

"That's what I mean," Colin explained, "the power of auto-suggestion. Pamela was told something awful would happen, and it did!"

What happened were several near-fatal car accidents. On approaching red traffic lights, the brakes completely failed and they were nearly killed. Yet immediately afterwards the brakes worked perfectly, and a check showed no mechanical defects. Colin has his own theory of what happened.

"There was never any evidence afterwards that anything was actually wrong. Therefore I must have been tricked into thinking I had applied the brakes, when in fact I had done no such thing."

Then, when giving Pamela a lift home from work, both of them sensed a 'presence' in the back of the car. Suddenly, Colin began gasping and choking as if he was being strangled, and the car started weaving about the road. Pamela controlled her panic, and retaliated in the best way she knew how. She recited the Lord's Prayer. It worked. Colin instantly recovered.

Could the materialisation of 'demonic entities' be explained by auto-suggestion, too ? Pamela answered for both of them.

"As Christians, we both know that demons do actually exist on a different 'plane' to ours. But these demons, when summoned, are capable of manifesting here. They can appear in any form, to a crowd of people, or remain invisible except to one person."

Pamela's encounter with such an entity was dramatic and horrifying.

"After the threats, I began keeping notes, just in case... Apart from being friends with Kay, the MD's secretary, the bond of Christianity also bound us together. She knew everything that had been going on. We arranged that, should anything happen at work, I would alert her by throwing a switch on the switchboard."

This particular day, Colin was on the phone telling her of a further incident involving the car. During the conversation she went cold.

"I was sitting at the reception desk, and as we talked, I noticed the figure of a man, forming out of nothing, across the room. I slowly put the phone down, and the figure, clothed in robes, came across to me. I managed to throw the switch, just as his hands closed around my throat."

9

Kay found her friend slumped semi-conscious across a chair on the far side of the room. When Colin heard of this, he immediately went to a meeting of the coven "to try and sort things out". They were ready for him. They had a "marvellous" revelation to bring to his notice, which would deter him from this "nonsense" of wanting to leave. Foolishly he agreed to undergo hypnotic regression, where he was allegedly taken back to several previous lives.

"Surprise, surprise, Pamela featured in several of my supposed previous incarnations. My mind flooded with imagery. In one scene we were in Aztec Mexico, thousands of years ago, as Priest and Priestess. Then I was shown pictures of France in the seventeenth century. Pamela was burnt at the stake and I was being hung. They convinced me these things had actually occurred. I went full circle. It was obvious, wasn't it ? Pamela belonged with me, and we belonged in the coven..."

Pamela took up the story.

"One night we were parked up, and he was insisting all this had happened to us. I was arguing with him, when suddenly I went very strange. I could hear Colin repeating, over and over; 'What can you see? What can you see?' I saw, something, a picture, and I described it to him. There was, I suppose you'd call her, a High Priestess of some kind, surrounded by her acolytes. Colin was saying; 'Look at her face, look at her face, who is she?' When I looked, it was me..."

In the lounge of their house, Colin leaned earnestly towards me.

"But that was me using auto-suggestion on Pamela, and it's not surprising that she began to waver. The idea that one has been incarnated throughout the centuries with the same partner in positions of supernatural power, must appeal to anyone with the least bit of romanticism in them."

But things were about to rush headlong towards a climax.

Not long after, Colin woke up one morning with terrible pains in his stomach. As he drove to Pamela's mother's house, he was feeling worse by the minute. He arrived at 10am, then... But there isn't a 'then' for Colin Hale. His mind remains blank of the dramatic occurrences of the next nine hours. But for Pamela, that day will remain etched in her memory forever.

"When he came into the house there was obviously something very wrong. He looked very strange, almost as if he was drugged. He sat down and stared around the room like a madman. After an hour or so of trying to make conversation, I decided I needed to get out of the house, and said I was going for cigarettes. Immediately, Colin stood up and offered to take me. What could I say?

"At the junction with the main road, he stopped the car, even though the way was clear. He sat as if waiting for something. He was. A lorry appeared, and as it drew closer, he turned the car into it. I grabbed the wheel and averted a collision. By now I was hysterical, but all I could hear from him, over and over again, was how he had to kill me and kill himself.

"Somehow I got us back to the house, and bundled him inside. There was something badly wrong and I was afraid for my mother's safety. I persuaded her to go across to a friend's house, but Colin followed me into the front garden, picked me up as if I was a rag doll, and flung me into the privet hedge."

This was some feat, as Colin is not a big man, but of slim build.

"Fortunately, I was only scratched, but like a fool, I followed him back inside. Thinking I had pacified him, we both sat down. I was wrong. Suddenly he shot up, body rigid as a board, arms out straight before him, face contorted. And the voice which came from his lips was not his. There was a terrible laugh - then he came for me.

"I backed out of the room, down the hallway until I reached the front door. His hands went for my neck, but I ducked and ran outside. It was two o'clock in the afternoon, people were stopping in the street to watch. Colin stood in the doorway like a zombie, arms out straight, screeching and laughing in that horrible voice.

"In a cry of sheer desperation I cried out; 'God help him, please help him!' Immediately, his arms dropped and his body toppled forwards off the steps. With a crack his head hit the concrete path below. I was convinced he must be dead, but when I turned him over there wasn't a scratch or a mark on him. My mother came rushing over, and we helped him inside."

She decided that after eighteen months of struggle, enough was enough. Alone, Pamela had lost the battle to break Colin's bond with witchcraft. There was only one course left. If he ever wanted to see her again he must have faith in her, she told him, and in her religion. After two hours of coaxing he eventually agreed. They took him to some Christian friends of hers, and at 7pm, the Reverend Ted Farmer arrived.

This is what he told me.

"Colin seemed to be in some sort of a trance - he didn't seem to be with it at all. I listened to Pamela's story, and became convinced he was possessed by an evil spirit. When people dabble in the occult, they become either oppressed or possessed. Most leave themselves wide open to possession.

"We all prayed for him, then laid hands on his body, asking if there was an evil spirit in possession, it should leave him in the name of Jesus Christ. I knew I was up against it. Suddenly I went into 'tongues'. This is a supernatural means of direct communication with God."

Pamela continued:

"Colin started thrashing, kicking, screaming. Then, after twenty minutes he seemed to calm down and revert to his original self. He clung to me and pleaded; 'don't leave me, please don't leave me.' Then it started again. At one point, several of us had to hold him down."

Colin does have a slender memory of what occurred next.

"I always wore around my neck a heavy metal ankth - an occult symbol - fastened by a leather cord. I have this vague memory of yanking it from around my neck and hurling it across the room."

Pamela described the immediate effect this action had.

"He let out a piercing scream, and for the first time that day, his body completely relaxed, his eyes opened and he recognised me."

Whatever had been in possession of Colin Hale's body had been successfully driven out. He described his feelings.

"I then realised what was going on. I felt like a naked one year-old waking up in the middle of a field. I didn't know where I was, what I was supposed to be doing. They were saying a few prayers. By this time I was fairly recovered. It was late now, and Ted Farmer said; 'come down and see me tomorrow'. The whole point of the exercise was to renounce witchcraft. Ted continued: 'Do you accept Christ ?' I said 'yes'. But I said 'yes' just like saying; 'alright, fair enough'. I felt desperate. I hadn't really a clue at the time to what I was saying 'yes' to. I thought it's all over now, that's it. I've said 'yes' so I must be a Christian !

"I went back to my hotel, and that night I had everything thrown at me. 'Things' kept materialising in the room; demons, people, frightening images, even the Devil himself was there at one stage. They were threatening and cajoling me, telling me I was as good as dead, that both Pamela and I were going to die. They gave me three months to live if I didn't change my mind.

"Obviously I couldn't sleep, but I closed my eyes tight, but every time I opened them, they were there. I was in a terrible mess next morning. I went down to Ted and said 'I've had a hell of a night, I've had enough.' We had a long chat, and I said that if this is going to keep happening, he could forget the whole thing ! He explained that the battle was won yesterday, and all I had to do was 'claim that victory - it's no use beating someone off,' he said ' then the next day surrendering.'

"This made no sense to me, and I told him so. I wanted a crucifix to hang around my neck, to ward these things off. He said: 'We don't have things like that; lucky charms! All you need to say is I claim this victory that Jesus Christ has won for me on the cross.'

"I thought; this Christianity's a bit weak. Where are the Big Guns? I really didn't take him on. I thought, what a waste of time!

"That night in the hotel I was absolutely shattered, having had no sleep during the past two days. I switched off the lights and got my head down. It started immediately. I didn't know what to do, I was becoming really desperate. After a couple of hours - somewhere between two and three in the morning - I decided to do what Ted the vicar had told me, but I couldn't remember the words! Something in the back of my mind said; 'just ask God. He's there, pray to Him.' I'd never prayed like that to God in my life. But I did, and immediately, Ted's words flooded back into my mind.

"'I claim the victory that Christ won for me on the cross'. There was a sound like an audio tape suddenly being run very fast - then nothing. I was absolutely dazed. The demons, the threatening voices, were all gone. Everything was totally quiet, peaceful, normal. I thought, perhaps, I should say 'thank you'. I felt very awkward, even though I was on my own. I was embarrassed about talking to someone I couldn't see.

"The following Friday I was on a high. It was as if I had been wearing a heavy army greatcoat for years, and suddenly it was gone. I was walking on air. I went down to Pamela's, and she had found me a flat to visit in Warrington. We called at Ted's on the way, and I admitted to him that despite what had happened, I still couldn't believe in God. Ted said; 'test Him, ask Him for a sign, your own little miracle.'

"We always took the same route to Warrington - through Winwick, past St Oswald's Church. There's a nice little story connected with the church involving a pig. This stems from the fact that there is a pig's face carved into one of the walls. For the past eighteen months we had stopped by the church occasionally, looking for this carving in vain. We had never been able to find it.

"As we came up to the traffic lights outside the church, I had an idea. I asked God to prove Himself by showing us the pig ! As we stopped at the lights on the hill, facing the church, I looked up, and even though we were some distance away I could see the pig as easily as if it was right in front of me. After parking up, we went and took a closer look. It was eleven in the morning, and we just stood there like a couple of lunatics laughing and laughing..."

Colin has no doubts of the dangers of becoming involved in witchcraft, no matter how innocent some people might argue it is.

"I got into witchcraft because I was bored. But it's like drugs. Once you're hooked you sink deeper and deeper. I was looking for excitement, but the excitement I have found since, in serving God, is vastly superior. One, or both of us, could easy have lost our lives - or worse."

Chapter Two

THE DARK AGES

*England, ah, faithless England, which the protection afforded
by it's seas rendered inaccessible to the Roman's, the faith of
the Saviour spread even there.* Jacques-Benigne Bossuet

In the previous chapter we read a very graphic account of a couple
who believe they have fought with occult forces generated by
malefic witchcraft. In order to understand the current conflict
between Christianity and occultism, it is necessary to go back to
the very roots of paganism itself.

'Pagan' is derived from the Latin, paganus, meaning 'coun-
tryman' - someone attuned intimately with nature, with a belief
in nature gods and spirits. Modern witches, who are also pagans,
worship the 'Goddess', the 'Earth Mother', known by many
names, but commonly called 'Diana'. 'She', they believe, cher-
ishes and nourishes those who show their love and obedience
through ritual and a deep respect for the Earth.

As soon as man was able to reason, he became a religious
animal. In Palaeolithic times he depicted that awareness in art,
in the creation of cult objects. During the Old Stone Age, an artist
of that time painted a picture on a cave wall in the Ariège region
of France: A man, clothed in skins and wearing antlers, is
dancing, surrounded by other animals. This is the earliest known
illustration of religious ritual. The horned figure, here clearly
suggesting origins as old as mankind himself, in later epochs
became a deity worshipped around the far-flung reaches of the

ancient world. In Britain he became Pan, and Herne the Hunter - supernatural denizens of the underworld. It is easy to see why man developed, with the ability to think, a religious cosmology of life and death, a grand tapestry of light and dark of which he was just one thread amongst the weave.

Man was surrounded by so much magic: The sun which brought light, warmth and growth; The ripe fruit of the trees and bushes; The beasts of the land, the creatures of the sea who helped sustain this fledgeling race; The seasons, analogous to the physical development of the individual; The waxing and waning of the moon - a twenty-eight day reprise at one with the menstrual cycle of the woman; a gift from the cosic tapestry weavers, the birth of a child; Its destiny - another bit of magic of time and place.

Mankind was the microcosm within the macrocosm. He saw himself enmeshed within a vast complex web of life and death forces. His reasoning told him something else, too. This did not just happen. It could not come about by accident. It was not just a thing of chance and circumstance. There must be superhuman beings at the controls somewhere who put this thing together. These supernatural entities must decide whether the crops failed or ripened, whether the tribe was barren or fertile, whether a man would rise to be a great leader or remain one of the masses.

The pagan priests saw and spoke to these heathen gods. Like modern mediums and psychics who claim to be channels for extraterrestrial and spiritual beings, they passed on messages and took orders. The gods had to be placated and worshipped according to various elaborate rituals, or else...

The rains would wash away the crops, children would be born mentally and physically crippled, plague, smallpox and polio would eat into the living fabric of the tribe. The moon goddess would turn her dark side towards them. If the gods were really angry, then the very earth itself would tremble with hurricane, tidal wave and earthquake. But who or what were these deities?

It is difficult to know in detail what the Ancient Britons worshipped. It was too long ago, and no written records were kept. But peoples the world over were developing a similar planetary awareness, and an awesome respect for the magical forces of nature. When the Angles, Saxons and Jutes rowed over to Britain from mainland Europe around 450 AD, they not only brought their farming skills, but their gods too: Tiw, Woden, Thunor, and the goddess, Frig.

Records kept elsewhere tell us that Frig was equivalent to the Roman Venus, a goddess of love and fertility. There are indications too, that the concept of the Earth Mother was worshipped in England at least as far back as 98 AD. The Great Goddess was venerated under a variety of titles in different parts of the world, two thousand years before Christ. And it is this essential matriarchal deity that most witches worship today.

The Goddess, Earth Mother and Lover, was a powerful symbol which could not be banished. Some commentators believe that it was because of this that the fledgeling Christian Church elevated Mary, mother of Jesus, to the Virgin Mary, Mother of God, at the Council of Ephesus in 431 AD. Popular historical writer, Geoffrey Ashe argues strongly the importance of this move to hyperdulia (super-veneration) of Mary. Without it, he says, Christianity would have dwindled to nullity.

One and a half centuries after England had been invaded by the Angles, Saxons and Jutes, there was another, altogether more subtle invasion - the invasion of Christianity.

Christianity had been introduced originally by the Romans in the second century, and after a period of success, had declined, until its eventual establishment following a new, more successful campaign in the seventh century. Missionaries arrived on the island in a concerted effort to convert the populace from their pagan gods and goddesses to the one masculine Christian God. It was not easy. They were fighting against centuries of ingrained heathenism. But the Christians were very clever, realising that brute force would only lead to prolonged warfare. They devised a short cut, which would convert the pagan English by subtly replacing their religion with Christianity.

This was only the start. By a gradual process, most of the pagan rituals and feast days were transformed into Christian celebrations. Paganism could not be completely eradicated, so it was decided to smother it instead.

Although 25 December was decreed the birthday of Christ in the fourth century, it was another five hundred years before the term 'Midwinter Feast' was replaced by 'Christmas' and Jesus Christ and the saints were adopted in favour of the pagan deities. This uneasy alliance trundled along until the Norman invasion of England in 1066 when the pagan celebration was restored, only for the Christian dimension to be re-installed with renewed vigour in the Middle Ages.

Beltane was a Celtic fire festival celebrated on 1 May to mark the beginning of summer. 'May Day' became superimposed on this ancient ritual and became a dramatised presentation of the union between spring and summer. All Hallows' Eve, or Hallowe'en, is another pagan ceremony that the Christians sought to eradicate by juxtaposing it with one of their own celebrations. Another north European Celtic tradition, it was the antithesis of Beltane. 1 November was a huge and glorious fire festival called Samhain, brought about to mark the beginning of winter and the reaping of crops impregnated with the spirit of fertility during the previous May Day.

But the evening before - 31 October - was also a festival of the dead and the powers of darkness, and is inextricably linked with contemporary witchcraft. The Church cannot forget that the old religion dictated that during the eve of Samhain, the souls of the dead returned from the grave to re-visit their homes. In order to counteract this, All Saints Day, first introduced in the seventh century, was moved from 13 May, to 1 November one hundred years later. The Roman Catholics have a similar 'All Souls Day' on 2 November, when prayers are said for the souls of the dead.

Just when did witchcraft emerge ? Is there a direct link with the ancient pagan religions as many occultists claim ? The witch cult is a global manifestation cutting across culture and class barriers. Our pagan forefathers, who worshipped the dark and light forces that controlled their lives, looked to the wise man of the tribe or temple priest for guidance in ritual and other matters, because of that person's supposed special relationship with those forces. Arguably the priest and vicar serve the same purpose in the Christian religion today.

The 'witch' was probably then a member of the tribe who had gained a superior knowledge of things, and was skilled in the use of the healing powers of herbs, and ritual ceremony. But is there a tradition of witchcraft which has continued down the centuries? Certainly modern practitioners of the Art claim that same direct intimacy with the forces of light and dark, and allege an ability to wield magic. Modern parapsychologists term such people 'psychic'. This psychism allegedly has the power, when combined with ritual, of calling down the old gods from their world into ours, of conjuring up white magic or black magic, which can heal or harm, save or kill...

By the end of the Dark Ages, the heirarchy of the relatively new religion of Christianity had decided to tolerate no longer its more ancient rival. But before a single 'witch' had been put to death, a macabre dress rehearsal had taken place in the conflict with other heretics, such as the Albigensians or Cathars who spread throughout southern France, Germany and northern Italy during the eleventh and twelfth centuries. They believed in a god of good, who had created the spiritual world and the spiritual being Jesus Christ, and a god of evil, who had created the material world. The evil god controlled the world, therefore, Jesus, the Son of God, could not have been a physical incarnation and the

Church of Rome, in believing in the literal interpretation of the New Testament, was founded on a lie.

After missionaries had failed to convert the Cathars by peaceful argument, Pope Innocent III declared war on them in 1208, and slaughtered thousands over the next two decades. Twenty thousand alone were massacred at Béziers; and two hundred at Montségur in the Pyrenees were put to the torch in enormous pyres. At the end of this period of savagery, the Catholic faith had gained such power and dominance that it would not countenance the least bit of opposition or competition from alternative religions.

Yet despite this power, there still remained the perennial thorn in the side of the Christian Church. Despite the success of Christianity the spectre of the old religion still bubbled beneath the surface of daily life, ingrained in the very fabric of medieval society. That was intolerable.

Curiously, a similar situation exists today in Latin America, particularly in Brazil. There, millions of Catholics also practice 'spiritism'. This is a variant of 'spiritualism', brought to Brazil by African slaves in the 19th century, and refined by a Frenchman called Alain Kardec. Here it has created no conflict. In fact, in 1957, spiritism was officially endorsed by the Brazilian government when they produced five million postage stamps portraying Kardec.

In the Middle Ages it was different. Paganism was outlawed when it was 'proven' with Biblical references that the old religion was the way in which 'the fallen angel' worked to capture and poison the human soul. The common people, with one foot in both camps, must have felt bogged down in a morass of double-think. Witchcraft researchers, Edgar Peel and Pat Southern, made the following observation:

> The attraction of the idea of a goddess - the comforting, embracing mother - is surely acknowledged by the prominence given to Mary by the Roman Catholic Church. Yet, while a place can be

21

found for a woman, the Christian God could brook no male rivals, and instead of being assimilated the god of the old religion became the Devil of the new, and the horned deity of the witches was identified with God's adversary, Satan, a possible origin of the idea that the Devil has horns.

The Church had been trying to put down fortune-telling and spell-peddling since the Dark Ages, but this new development in Christian orthodoxy gave impetus to a more violent conflict. It meant that anyone practising paganism was carrying out the work of the Devil, and by implication set to challenge the Christian God. Almost overnight these uneasy bedfellows were hastened into bloody conflict. In the terror that followed, Catholic, and later Protestant witchfinders, created a bloodbath in which most of the victims were their own kind. The twin-headed hydra of State and Religion rampaged through the streets of towns, villages and cities. In this distorted perversion of Christian values, it did not seem a high price to pay for the extermination of those who would worship other gods and goddesses.

Perhaps the most famous witch of all to be tried and then burnt at the stake, was Joan of Arc. This Maid of Orléans, daughter of a well-to-do peasant in fifteenth-century France, appeared to be an extraordinary clairvoyant and clairaudient. She had premonitions, and from the age of thirteen, claimed to hear voices under a 'fairy tree', close to her home. These voices, which she believed belonged to St Gabriel, St Michael, St Margaret and St Catherine, encouraged her to remain virginal and pure of thought. Later, when news reached the district of Lorraine that Orléans was under siege by the English, these same voices ordered her to save the city !

The rest, as they say, is history. She did indeed relieve Orléans and many other towns - sending the English invaders to flight. But on the 23 May 1430, she was captured outside the walls of Compiègne and sold to the English by the Burgundian commander.

Joan became the star in a huge show-trial designed to discredit Charles VII of France. At the centre of the debate was the argument; were Joan's psychic powers really from God, or were they diabolic ? Was the virgin heroine of France a witch ?

For political reasons the conclusion was pre-ordained and skilfully brought about by the inquisitors who successfully 'proved' their case in a way which was to become familiar to thousands of others across Europe and beyond. Joan of Arc was burnt at the stake as a witch on 30 May 1431. Her own people never lifted a finger to save her, and in true ecclesiastical fashion, in 1456 the decision arrived at twenty five years earlier was annulled. In 1909 Joan was beatified and then, in 1920, canonised by the Roman Catholic Church. The witch was now a saint!

But the atrocity which set the pattern for all future persecutions took place near the city of Arras, north of Paris, in 1459. A hermit, charged with heresy, was tortured and sent to the stake. Under torture he implicated a prostitute and a respected elderly poet. These too 'confessed' and in turn implicated others, who were also arrested, and so on and so on... Researcher Francis X. King describes this cycle of arrest, torture, confession, denunciations and more arrests, "like some ghastly pyramid-selling operation."

These executions snowballed until they affected even the commercial running of the city. No one could be certain whether or not the merchant they were dealing with might at any moment be arrested and his wealth confiscated. Arras became isolated while the purge continued.

At the centre of it all were two Dominican friars who conducted the inquisition with fanatical fervour. Their paranoid beliefs incorporated the opinion that many bishops and cardinals practised witchcraft, and up to one third of the population of Christian Europe were secret witches. With profound logic, they reasoned that anyone who opposed the execution of witches must therefore be a follower of Satan themselves! This philosophy was the precedent for witch purges for the next two hundred years or more.

The condemned citizens of Arras went to the stake pronouncing their innocence to their fellow citizens. They claimed their alleged confessions were induced under torture and it was lies that they worshipped the Devil and attended Sabbats. The inquisitors had told them that if they 'confessed', their only penance would be a short pilgrimage. But they were burned anyway.

The Duke of Burgundy, learning of this cruel fiasco, decreed that all future interrogations must be carried out in the presence of one of his heralds. Despite continued pressure from the Dominican friars, there were no more arrests. An investigation of the original atrocity was concluded after thirty years, when the victims of the fire were posthumously exonerated.

Just a few years before this decision was reached in France, another weapon had been added to the arsenal of oppression. The pen is indeed mightier than the sword, and nothing was more devastating than the *Malleus Maleficarum*. This 'Hammer of Evil' became the bible of the judiciary. Written by two German Dominicans, Heinrich Kramer and Jakob Sprenger, under encouragement by the Pope; it told in a quarter of a million words everything which was known, or imagined, about witchcraft. In its final section it explained procedures for the trial, torture and punishment of those accused.

To the judiciary, executioners and the Church, the *Malleus* was heaven sent. Between 1486 and 1520, at least fourteen editions were printed. From 1584, six English editions appeared. This new work quickly replaced the *Canon Episcopalis* - a document which up until the thirteenth century reflected the Church's belief that the powers endowed upon witches were purely imaginary.

One of the vital components of the terror was the part played by children. Many were tortured and executed, but others were granted immunity from prosecution provided they implicated their elders. It is surprising, whatever the base truth of such allegations, how the inquisitors swallowed every nuance of absurdity handed to them.

Protestants, such as Calvin, drove the witch hunts to new heights, by claiming that the Devil was re-doubling his efforts in the territories of the Reformed Churches. In Geneva, hundreds were arrested and tortured, and thirty four executed in less than a year during the 1540s and, in 1566, the first Englishman was hanged. But by far the worst atrocities were to be committed in Germany - more than three hundred years before the Nazis carried out the torture, imprisonment and extermination of six million Jews.

German burghermaster Johannes Junius and thousands of others accused of witchcraft, suffered weeks of torture before they were eventually hanged or burned at the stake. Junius died on 6 August, 1628, not long after smuggling this letter out to his daughter:

> And then came also - God in the highest heaven have mercy - the executioner, and put the thumbscrews on me, both hands bound together, so that the blood spurted from the nails and everywhere, so that for four weeks I could not use my hands, as you can see from my writing.
>
> Thereafter they stripped me, bound my hands behind me, and drew up on the ladder. Then I thought heaven and earth was at an end. Eight times did they draw me up and let me fall again, so that I suffered terrible agony. I said to Dr Braun: "God forgive you for misusing an innocent." He replied: "You are a knave"...
>
> Now, my dearest child, you have all my acts and confessions, for which I must die. And it is all sheer lies and inventions, so help me God...If God send no means of bringing the truth to light, our whole kindred will be burned...

He was accused, along with four colleagues, of worshipping Satan, having sexual intercourse with a succubus - a female demon - desecrating the sacred host and riding to a witches' sabbat on the back of a black dog. The devilish insanity which swept across Europe, Britain and her colonies in North America, perverted the judicial machine into a sadistic steamroller which crushed in its path between 200,000 and nine million men, women and children. This savagery, instigated by powerful elements within the Christian Church, became a huge industry lining the pockets and fattening the bellies of judges, witchfinders, jailors, executioners, torturers, clerks and merchants who provided the scaffolding and wood for the fires.

Although witch trials began in the mid-fifteenth century, the bulk date from 1570, during the Counter Reformation of the Roman Catholic Church. In thirteen years, three hundred alleged sorcerers were executed in the state of Bamburg alone, irrespective of age or sex. Many children died at the hands of the Catholics. From 1623 until 1632 Bamburg became known as 'the shrine of horror', ruled by the fanatical Prince Bishop Gottfried von Dornheim. This 'witch bishop' set up what in a future time were called 'concentration camps'. In the seventeenth century they were termed *Hexenhausen*, or Witches Houses. These were nothing more than processing plants. However, it was not food or manufacturing materials which were processed, but the minds and flesh of living human beings. Prisoners entered the *Hexenhaus* at one door and exited at another, weeks, months later. Broken in both body and spirit, maimed almost beyond recognition, they would suffer their final release in the flames of the pyre.

Although the great witch purge spanned a continent and crossed the seas to Britain and North America, nothing matched the cruelty exhibited by the Germans. Torture was prohibited in England except by a special act of Parliament. Burnings did take place in Scotland, but hanging by and large was the punishment for English witches. Even though England never entered into the swing of things as much as her neighbours, people were arrested just the same, 'persuaded' to confess and executed. Although torture was not part of the English constitution, pressure was applied in more subtle ways.

Suspects were 'swum'. This meant the victim's arms and legs were shackled together, then they were tossed into a river. If they sunk they were innocent, if they floated it was deemed that invisible demons were supporting them, and guilt was confirmed. Often the filthy damp and freezing conditions in which alleged witches were kept during months of interrogation was enough to bring about a confession. Sometimes suspects were just worn down, until, exhausted, they would confess just for release.

A case in point is that of the Revd John Lowe, an elderly vicar of the Suffolk parish of Brandeston. Witchfinder General, Matthew Hopkins, subjected this poor man to the 'walking torture'. He was made to walk for days on end until his feet bled and he fainted with exhaustion. Hopkins had a team of 'walkers' who were organised into shifts to keep the seventy year-old man on the move. Other suspects were made to run in this way. Eventually the vicar made the bizarre confession that he had caused an imp to sink a ship out at sea. Although no check was made to see if such a vessel even existed, never mind whether it was sunk, John Lowe was hanged after reading out his own burial service. Witchcraft itself was not a capital punishment, but murder through sorcery was.

Matthew Hopkins carved out quite a successful career for himself in East Anglia between 1644 and 1646, on the tail end of the civil war. A former lawyer, he managed to get four witches hanged after claiming they had sent a demon to murder him in the garden of his house. Hopkins walked the fine line between psychological and physical pressures, and illegal torture. Such was the fear he instilled by his very presence that people often confessed without any pressure being applied at all. Hundreds were imprisoned at his behest and something like two hundred persons were hanged before this Witchfinder General fell from glory. It was during his incursions into Huntingdon that Hopkins came into conflict with a clergyman called Revd John Gaule. The parson attacked him from the pulpit and produced a pamphlet exposing the tortures used by the former lawyer and his cronies. Twelve months earlier, John Gaule might have suffered a similar fate to John Lowe, but the times were changing. Matthew Hopkins was forced to retire with his wealth to his home in Manningtree, where, twelve months later, he died of tuberculosis.

Witch hunts had been slow to take off in England because of a book called *Discoverie of Witchcraft* by Reginald Scot. This exposed such trials for their lack of proper evidence and absurd quality of confession. Scot published the book two years after the St Osyth trials of 1582. There, fourteen women were charged with various acts of witchcraft on the say-so of children between six and nine years old. But *Discoverie*, written in plain English instead of Latin, was attacked by Puritan ministers and by King James VI of Scotland, who, in 1597, produced his *Demonology*. This became the guide book for magistrates, lawyers and witchfinders. When James took over the English throne in 1604, he passed a new, more severe, Witchcraft Act to replace the one of 1563 and ordered all copies of Reginald Scot's book to be burnt.

Probably the best documented witch trials were those of nineteen men and women at Lancashire Assizes in 1612. What began as a series of disputes between villagers in Pendle Forest, escalated into tragedy.

The story began in 1595, when Christopher Nutter and his son, Robert, died within a short time of one another. The family claimed they had been bewitched by an old woman called 'Chattox' and her daughter, Alizon, who lived with several other family members in a humble abode on land owned by the Nutters. These were the first of sixteen alleged witchcraft deaths to emerge during judicial inquiries about eighteen years later.

A few miles away lived another elderly lady, known as 'Old Demdike', together with her son-in-law, John Device, and his family. They also had a reputation for using witchcraft. The trouble started when the two families came into conflict. There were many murmurings and complaints concerning both families and their alleged witchcraft practices for many months. But the incident which attracted the authorities took place outside Pendle Forest, near Colne, on 18 March 1612.

Alizon was travelling along the road to Trawden when she met a pedlar called John Law. The young woman asked him for some pins, but either because she had no money, or because he was too obstinate, he refused to undo his pack. Alizon became angry with him, and as he turned away, Law suffered a stroke. He was taken to a nearby ale-house, speechless, and subsequently, his son, Abraham, arrived from Halifax. Alizon was found, and the pedlar, now with his speech regained, accused her of bewitchment. Alizon admitted that this was the case, but begged forgiveness, which was given by the victim. However, the son was not satisfied, and on 30 March, he, together with Alizon, went up before a magistrate called Roger Nowell. Alizon described what had happened, adding that a black dog had appeared beside her which spoke in English:

"What wouldst thou have me to do unto yonder man ?"

"What canst thou do to him ?" Alizon asked.

"I can lame him." The dog said.

"Lame him !" She said gleefully.

John Law had not gone two hundred yards before he collapsed.

Alizon went on to describe her initiation into witchcraft by her grandmother. She had met the familiar of the black dog some time before, which had taken her soul by sucking on her body below the breasts. Then examples emerged of witchcraft deeds carried out by Chattox and Demdike, implicating both families. Arrests were made, and witch's marks were discovered on several of them. Neighbours were found to testify against them. In particular, Mother Demdike, old, lame and blind - a classic fairytale witch - came in for a lot of attention. Thomas Potts was the clerk at the Assizes who recorded the trial, and in 1613 published a book, *The Wonderfull Discoverie Of Witches In The Countie Of Lancaster*.

Demdike explained to Nowell how, twenty years ago, she had met the Devil in the form of a boy, half his coat black, half brown. In exchange for her soul, he had promised to help her acquire things she wished for. The Devil subsequently appeared as a brown dog, black cat and a hare, and was called 'Tibb'. Tibb, according to Demdike, helped her to kill people through supernatural means. Demdike then explained how victims were maimed or killed using 'sympathetic magic', the use of a small doll representing the victim during rituals.

Demdike then implicated Chattox, who in turn described how a spirit called 'Fancie' made a deal regarding her soul, then aided and abetted her in bringing about the deaths of Christopher and Robert Nutter.

After some twenty witches had assembled at Malkin Tower to discuss what was happening, Jennet Device, who had also been present, was later persuaded to give evidence against her own relatives and friends! Jennet was just nine years old...

Gradually, members of both families were sucked into the vortex, together with witches outside Pendle, from places like Padiham, St Helens and Samlesbury. More supernatural murders came to light, together with lesser crimes of livestock killing, graveyard robbing, milk and beer souring. Finally, in August, nineteen witches went up for trial at Lancaster Assizes. All but one pleaded 'Not Guilty.' They were tried before a jury, although none of the accused were allowed to prepare a defence. Most of the Lancashire witches died on the gallows, several strangled to death, watched by the crowds who had flocked to see them.

If the trials of the Lancashire witches were well documented, then so was the phenomenal witch craze which temporarily took over Salem Village, now Danvers, Massachusetts.

This was strong Puritan country, so when eleven year-old Abigail Williams and twelve year-old Ann Putnam went into fits, and started acting like animals, the local community was horrified. Things reached crisis point when the hysteria spread across the female juvenile population. The girls claimed they were bewitched. Eventually, at the end of February 1692, Abigail and Ann gave the village minister - a Mr Samuel Parris - three names belonging to their tormentors. Two of them were women who were unpopular in Salem, but the third, Parris' West Indian slave, Tituba, had struck up a close relationship with the girls. It was assumed that Tituba had talked to them of voodoo and other African witchcraft practices.

The two American women denied they were witches, but Tituba readily confessed, and furthermore - surprise, surprise - implicated others as instruments of the Devil. The girls went into paroxysms at the sound of these new names. Many arrests followed, and no fewer than fifty executions occurred.

It soon became clear that anyone could be tested for Devil worship by being brought into close proximity to the affected girls. If the girls went into a fit, the test was positive. People who were brave or foolhardy enough to cast doubts on the whole affair brought suspicion down on themselves, as had happened in Europe. One of these was the deputy constable, John Willard. He refused to make any more arrests - and was executed himself.

By September, the death toll was twenty, and two hundred people were being held in Boston and Salem prison. Many more would have been arrested, including the Governor's wife and the president of Harvard, but there was no more prison accommodation available. Conditions in the cramped prisons must have been awful, but one case in particular was extremely cruel: Little five year-old Dorothy Good was chained, along with her mother, in a dungeon. The woman was eventually hanged, and the pathetic child mentally deranged by the experience.

Some suspects were bound tightly at the heels and neck until blood burst from their noses. Others, who would not recognise the court, and refused to plead, could legally be induced to recognise the indictment. This was the case with an accused witch called Giles Corey. Corey was eighty years of age, but this did not stop the Salem authorities from 'pressing' him.

The old man was laid out on the cell floor, and heavy weights were placed on his body until he either pleaded and the trial could begin, or he died. Giles Corey suffered the excruciating pain of being slowly pressed, and chose to die instead.

The madness only ended when Governor Phips, who had been away from the colony for most of the summer, returned, and cancelled the special commission which had been set up. The ordinary courts acquitted those in custody, and Phips pardoned the rest. As if waking from a nightmare, those who had carried out the persecutions realised the full horror of that long bloody summer of 1692. The summer, when the Devil, it seemed, having finished with his work elsewhere, crossed an ocean to bring inhuman suffering and degradation through the hands and minds of the Puritan citizens of New England.

Why were thousands, possibly millions, roasted alive or publicly strangled after suffering weeks and months of the most horrible tortures imaginable? Why were whole communities wiped out; wives, husbands, brothers, sisters, sons and daughters - stripped of all dignity, raped of all humanity? Why was the very fabric of society stained with the blood of its citizens by those who administered and controlled it? Is there a fundamental lesson here which has not been learnt?

There was another witch hunt during the 1950s. Senator Joe McCarthy, the Witchfinder General of post war American society, was instrumental in hunting down and destroying the lives of hundreds of men and women whom he labelled 'communists'.

People were sacked, careers ruined, marriages broken and the suicide rate rocketed up. Ironically, McCarthy's methods aped those of the people he most hated and feared - the Russians. They in turn were a reflection of the methodology used in the witch craze three centuries before. In Soviet Russia, people were encouraged to spy on their friends and report relatives who disagreed with communist doctrine to the KGB. Although those convicted were not burnt at the stake, they were tortured, sent to psychiatric hospitals or forced labour camps and sometimes shot. Only now can we begin to think of these inhumanities in the past tense.

Why this genocide occurred both in the Middle Ages and in modern times is as clear as the screams that penetrated the stone walls of the torture chambers: politics, power, money, sadism and religious or ideological intolerance, and, some have argued; genuine malefic witchcraft.

But the backbone of the entire witch-hunting movement were extremists within the Christian Church. They alone convinced the bureaucrats that the old religion was the Devil's religion, founded by the fallen angel, Lucifer, and anyone who practised fortune-telling or was especially skilled in 'magical' herbal cures or lived alone and was known to curse people, must be a witch. It was, therefore, the duty of a Christian society to search out such cancers and eradicate them completely. To encourage the muscle of the state to act speedily and with the utmost force, it was stated often and vigorously that witchcraft was not only found throughout society, it was on the increase.

There were a lot of Christians who believed this, and reasoned that the ends justified the means. Christians who argued against what was happening found themselves on the receiving end of the thumb screws and hangman's noose. But was this the case everywhere ? Did the Church 'invent' witchcraft in order to eradicate a competitive belief system ? If so, it is a heavy cross which Christianity bears.

In the case of Salem, this interpretation is challenged by author Chadwick Hansen, in his book, *Witchcraft At Salem*. Hansen did some original research and studied actual documents surviving from that time. Many of these are quoted in the text, showing, he says, that the clergy were against the witchcraft trials, particularly 'spectral evidence'. Those afflicted with fits in proximity to alleged witches, were harmed, they said, by the invisible 'spectres' of the accused. The clergy tried to deter the magistrates from handing out the death sentence, and pointed out that much of the evidence was faulty both in the way it was obtained and also in content. In Salem, at least, it was the will of the people which dictated that the trials must go on. Hansen is of the opinion that but for the intervention of the Puritan Church, there would have been many more deaths.

Historians have no belief in the supernatural. Perhaps this explains why it is often accepted that all the thousands of 'witches' put to death were either completely innocent, or self-deluded persons.

The case of Isobel Gowdie was most likely an example of fantasy taking on the proportions of subjective reality, according to most commentators. Although the late Dr Margaret Murray saw her 'confessions' as accounts of pagan religious celebrations, the richness and abundant diversity of their content lead most other researchers to conclude they were mental fantasies and no more. But that may not be the whole story.

Gowdie was a Scottish farmer's wife who approached the Elders of the kirk in 1662, informing them that for the previous fifteen years she had served the Devil. An attractive red-headed girl, life on the farm was boring, a condition reinforced by her childlessness and a husband who was her social and intellectual inferior. She claimed that after meeting a 'man in grey', he baptised her as a witch in Auldearne church. Things picked up then. She took part in wild orgies where she had sexual intercourse with various demons including the Devil himself. She was able to transform herself into a hare or a cat, could fly and reduce herself to the size of an insect. Colin Wilson, in his book, *The Occult*, remarks on the sexual obsessiveness of her confessions. It is not absolutely clear what happened to Mrs Gowdie, but it is safe to assume she was executed.

Did witches really exist ? Certainly it was believed that witches existed. And as we have already seen, some of those arrested sincerely swore they did practice witchcraft. But does this answer the question ?

Chadwick Hansen went against the grain when he produced documents which apparently showed that some of those persecuted in Salem were not just the innocent victims of bigotry. They were practising occultists who were not above using their 'powers' to harm their neighbours. Amongst those were Bridget Bishop, 'Candy' - a negro slave, Wilmot Redd, the Reverend George Burroughs, and Dorcas Hoare. This latter, Hansen is reasonably certain, was responsible for the death of a twelve year-old girl by witchcraft.

But the net cast out into the sea of humankind was indiscriminate. By the law of averages it must have caught a few sharks, but many more small fry were tragically swept up in its mesh.

Witches did exist and do today. White witches and occultists claim they are the bearers of the Ancient Religion - practised long before Christ was born. But is it an independent religion with as much validity as Christianity, or is it the Anti-Christ, the Anti-Good, the Anti-Man, the Anti-Matter of the positive universe created by a benevolent God ? A thing founded by the fallen 'angel' Lucifer, using the minds and souls of men as pawns in a hidden war. Were the Christian witchfinders right after all ? Further more, are today's witch hunters justified in their current campaign against modern paganism and its off-shoots? Are the questions posed in medieval times any more answerable in the declining years of the twentieth century ?

We know that for every 'positive' there is a 'negative'. One of the laws of physics states that for every action there is an equal and opposite reaction. Where there is Good there is Evil. Where there is God there is the Devil.

If God does exist then so does Satan. Is he the true deity behind the witch cult ?

Chapter Three

THEN...

Are you sitting comfortably ? Then I' ll begin. Julia S. Lang

In 1954, a book appeared which many saw as the catalyst of the re-birth of Wicca. *Witchcraft Today* was written by a retired civil servant, Gerald Gardner. The book was much more widely read than anyone would have imagined, and interest in this ancient pagan religion mushroomed. Was this, at last, the surfacing of a cult which persecution had driven underground for three hundred years? Or was it, as many critics pronounced, merely the eccentricities of an old man given form through public imagination? If witchcraft was not a re-invention, there should be evidence of some sort of continuity from medieval times until that watershed year of 1954.

Certainly prior to this date, the public still perceived witchcraft as a reality, and many believed that covens met in secret to carry out their 'blasphemous' rituals in celebration of the Moon Goddess and the Horned Nature God. Unofficially, suspects were still tested for their religious alignment through trial by ordeal. A Suffolk man was 'swum' in 1826 and a fortune-teller almost drowned when he suffered the same fate thirty six years later. The most extraordinary evidence that witchcraft was alive and well emerged nine years before Gerald Gardner's book, when it seems that an entire village may have conspired to cover up the murder of a man involved in sorcery.

Lower Quinton, a few miles south of Stratford upon Avon, sits in the shadow of Meon Hill, close to the Rollright Stones, reputedly older than Stonehenge. The area is steeped in witchcraft, and surrounded by place names such as Devil's Elbow, Upper and Lower Slaughter.

Charles Walton, a hedger and ditcher, had something of a sinister reputation in the village. He lived in a thatched cottage with his niece, and his next-door-neighbour shopped for him. Loners in small rural communities attract suspicion and gossip as a matter of course, but Walton, unwittingly it seemed, courted the darker emotions of his neighbours.

Outwardly he was just a labourer who did work for several local farmers, but during research for his book *Murder By Witchcraft*, Donald McCormick discovered some unusual things about Walton. Apparently this grizzle-haired droopy-moustached loner bred huge toads. One local inhabitant told him that Walton took to harnessing the toads to a miniature plough which was let loose on seeded fields. Isobel Gowdie had described, three hundred years earlier, this as the same method she used in order to magically stunt the growth of crops. Had the old man fallen out with one of his neighbours ?

It was claimed that Walton could imitate the call of every bird in the neighbourhood - and understood every word they said. Walton described how birds would perch on his hands and shoulders, flying off to any place he indicated with his hands. But, although he was supposed to have some control over animals, the sight of a black dog would send a chill of fear through him. This stemmed from a frightening boyhood experience: For three consecutive nights he had seen a phantom dog running across Meon Hill. On the third night he watched in terror as it transformed into a headless woman. The following morning his sister died. This changed him from an outgoing talkative young man into a brooding introvert.

Unfortunately for the elderly Charles Walton, or because of him, the year of 1944 was a bad one for the villagers of Lower Quinton. Despite an early spring, crops had been slow in growing and there had been several mishaps with livestock. Beer was of poor quality in the local pubs, and the harvest was every bit as bad as had been expected. Did someone blame this state of affairs on the alleged witchcraft practices of an old man? Curiously, the entire affair echoed an incident which occurred seventy years earlier in a neighbouring village...

In 1875, a seventy five year-old woman was murdered by a man called John Heywood, in Long Compton. The community had suffered a series of misfortunes, and Ann Tenant had become a focus for blame. Heywood, referred to as a village idiot, believed there was a coven operating in the village, and given the chance, he admitted, he would have killed them all:

"Her was a proper witch. I pinned Ann Tenant to the ground before slashing her throat with a bill-hook in the form of a cross," he confessed. Indeed, the poor woman had been pinned to the ground by a pitchfork.

On 14 February 1945, Walton was discovered on his back under a willow tree, a pitchfork driven through his neck with such force it had pierced the ground beneath to a depth of six inches. A cross had been carved from the neck to the lower abdomen, and the bill-hook which had been used to carry out the job was still wedged between his ribs. The parallels between the two murders are plain to see. But this was not just a murder, it had all the hallmarks of a pagan sacrifice.

It was believed that a witch's power source lay in her blood. A lot of suspected witches were 'blooded' - cut to release their 'supernatural' powers. Unfortunately, the release of blood often meant the release of life too, as in the case of Walton and Ann Tenant. 14 February was not only St Valentine's Day and Ash Wednesday, but also the date when the ancient Druids carried out sacrifices to ensure good crops. Colin Wilson speculated that the old man's murder was probably planned months in advance, to undo the damage he had supposedly done through the practice of evil ritual. Could Walton have been sacrificed by someone with pagan beliefs? Certainly it was someone with occult knowledge who was familiar with the earlier murder.

No-one was ever convicted of the killing. Detective Superintendent Robert Fabian of Scotland Yard and his team took four thousand statements and sent twenty nine samples of blood, hair and skin to police laboratories for analysis, but to no avail. The locals were less than helpful. A few days after the murder, a black dog was found hanged on Meon Hill. Did someone believe the animal was Charles Walton's familiar? Fabian himself saw a farm hand chasing a black dog which ran out of sight, but the boy denied there had been a dog. A police car ran over a dog, and other animals began to die during the police investigation.

It was, to say the least, a rum affair. Walton was not the victim of a casual killer, but possibly the focus of a successful attempt to purge the village of a practising witch who had allegedly carried out evil against his neighbours. At least that was what Dr Margaret Murray and others thought. If so, the clandestine witchfinders of Lower Quinton knew exactly how to cleanse the area of such 'Devil' worshippers. All this happened in 1945 - but it might just as well have been 1645. Was Walton, like most of those who had gone before him, an innocent eccentric who happened to be in the wrong place at the wrong time?

During research for this book I visited Lower Quinton. Before I entered the village, my gaze was drawn to the brooding slopes of Meon Hill - the sacrificial altar for the life of Charles Walton. Its patchwork skirt and wooded dome swathed in mist were an arresting sight.

The village is in two parts, Lower and Upper Quinton. It is made up of beautiful cotswold cottages, a duck pond and parish church, with a modern housing estate stuck clumsily onto its periphery. I went into the College Arms and ordered half a pint of bitter, telling the girl behind the bar that I was researching a book on witchcraft, and was interested in information on Walton.

"The man found dead on Meon, you mean?"

It could have happened yesterday. I nodded and she disappeared returning a minute later.

"Sorry, no-one here knows anything."

Is there anyone in the village surviving from that time, I asked?

"Only a few old men and they won't talk."

Should I try the vicarage?

"You could. They might have some old records."

I finished my beer and left.

While I had been in the pub church bells had begun to peal. I saw why. Guests were arriving in their finery for a wedding. That put the blocks on that idea, so I made my way up a narrow street braced with cottages and through the doors of the Gay Pig. A pleasant young lady smiled at me from the other side of the bar, and I explained once again why I was there. She carried on smiling as she disappeared into the back, and I had the impression she knew just the person I should speak to. When she returned her face was sullen.

"They don't know anything - anything at all. They've not been here long enough."

There was no doubt about it. The matter was firmly closed. Almost half a century later people were as uncooperative as when the police investigation was underway and McCormick himself was asking questions. I wandered around wondering what to do next and took a narrow lane out of the village. It was then I came across the British Legion Social Club. I hesitated, shrugged, then went inside. After hearing my request, the plump barlady called over a middle-aged man seated at a table. We went outside and chatted. He would not be identified but talked easily enough.

"I was only three at the time it happened, but I remember all the trouble it caused. There were so many rumours going around then, and since, that it's very difficult to decide exactly what the truth is. There did seem to be a feud between Walton and another man, called Potter, but if he did it, the police couldn't prove it, and he went to the grave with the secret. The witchcraft connection came about partly because a relative of Walton's had been burned as a witch in a nearby village during the Middle Ages.

"For years after, Detective Inspector Fabian used to hide up on Meon Hill on the anniversary of the killing. He was working on the theory that a murderer always returns to the scene of the crime. No-one ever did turn up, and some of the locals used to give him the run around in the pubs. You should try the Gay Pig. They know all about it there."

I told him of my reception at the Gay Pig and he gave me a knowing smile. I asked him if he knew which cottage in the village Walton and his niece had occupied. He was not sure.

As I walked back towards the church, I thought once more of talking to the vicar, and again I was thwarted. The service was now over, but wedding guests together with the Reverend Gerwyn James were streaming across the road and into the College Arms for the reception. I thought I would take a look around the graveyard. As I stepped up the path towards the beautiful stone church, the verger, a lady whom I took to be his wife, and a younger couple were just coming out. The younger lady smiled at me and said "Hello". I asked them where the grave of Charles Walton lay. The older woman fixed me with a hard stare, and said:

"Are you a reporter?"

I hastily assured her I was not, adding that I was a writer, researching a book on witchcraft. She was placated with this.

"You know, there's been an awful lot of rubbish written about Charlie Walton. All that stuff about the villagers not helping the police!"

But his murderer was never found, I interjected. She gave me a cold stare, so I changed the subject towards the witchcraft angle.

"That all came about because of that woman who came up from London, Murray something or other."

Dr Margaret Murray, I supplied.

"You see, the police were getting nowhere with their investigation, so she came up and said she had uncovered all these things to do with witchcraft. I don't see it myself, but there you are."

I asked again about the grave, but none of them knew which one it might be, the verger, adding:

"There was no headstone, you see."

Yes, I said, he was only a farm labourer, wasn't he?

"He lived over there, in that cottage," the old lady added.

I could not believe my luck. I must have walked past Walton's cottage some half dozen times in the past two hours. And there it was, right opposite the church, his present and permanent abode.

Was Charles Walton's death a ritual killing connected with local witchcraft? It is not clear. However one cannot be blind to the connections, and one cannot ignore the impression that even today, forty five years later, most of the villagers will not converse with outsiders. Certainly the case made a lasting impression on Fabian. In 1976, now in retirement, he commented to Charles Sandell of the *News Of The World*:

"Detectives deal in facts, but I must admit there was something uncanny about that investigation."

There is no clear cut evidence that witchcraft did survive the witch-hunting holocaust to go underground with greatly reduced numbers. The subject abounds with legends and rumours of covens and witch families existing in secrecy over the decades, although, understandably, there is very little hard evidence. Certainly people never lost their fear and belief in such practices. A few, like the fictional Van Helsing in Bram Stoker's *Dracula*, were even prepared to search out and bring down retribution on the heads of the Unchristians - even into the twentieth century.

Certainly the conflict between paganism and Christianity never died, and it is this conflict which we are primarily concerned with. It was not until 1951 that the 1736 Witchcraft Act was abolished. In this easier atmosphere the likes of Gerald Gardner, and later, Alec Sanders not only revived the ancient cult but brought to it hundreds, perhaps thousands, of new adherents.

Gardner himself claimed he came into contact with a coven of witches in the late 1930s, operating in the New Forest, and was initiated in 1946. At that time, the climate was not liberal enough to allow pro-witchcraft books to be published, so Gardner had to content himself with revealing some of the Craft's practices in the guise of a novel, *High Magic's Aid*. Then came *Witchcraft Today* followed by *The Meaning of Witchcraft*. Both books attracted a much wider audience than had been imagined, and upset a few witches because it was felt that they revealed a little too much.

With the help of an acolyte, Doreen Valiente, the former civil servant produced a manual called the *Book of Shadows*. This was built around a shell of hand-written manuscripts containing rituals and lore supposedly passed down from witch to witch, which Gardner re-modelled and added to. Some commentators have found a sexual and masochistic obsessiveness to the work. Certainly he borrowed from the writings of Aleister Crowley and from Freemasonry. But it proved popular and has since been plagiarised by other covens. Gardner loved the publicity that Fleet Street generated for him, and died in 1964, aged eighty.

Gardner was born near Liverpool, and although his father was a timber merchant and Justice of the Peace, was something of a self-made man. He travelled extensively and absorbed a wealth of knowledge which he put to good use during his Wiccan 'career'. But he was also a romanticiser. His professional and academic qualifications were a fraud, and his split with Doreen Valiente was brought about by one untruth too many.

Doreen Valiente cites Aleister Crowley - 'The Great Beast 666' - or rather John Symonds' biography of him, as also being instrumental in the witchcraft revival. Crowley was labelled by the press as being 'the wickedest man in the world' for his depraved rituals involving sexual magic, drugs and alcohol. Valiente says of him:

> Crowley may have been a brilliant writer and a splendid poet but as a person he was simply a nasty piece of work. His great importance in the occult world was that he had wrenched open that treasure chest in which the Order of the Golden Dawn had locked up the secret knowledge of the Western Mystery Tradition, and had invited all to share it.

Carrying the torch after Gardner was the self-styled 'King of the Witches', Alec Sanders. It was rumoured that Sanders had once trained to be a priest. His brand of witchcraft was an offshoot of Gardnerism, although basically in the Gardner tradition. Alec, and his young wife Maxine, made newspaper headlines in the footsteps of their 'master'. In the late sixties and early seventies, the couple initiated a large number of people into the cult, including Janet and Stuart Farrar - authors of several contemporary books on the subject.

Sanders claimed to have been initiated into witchcraft, however, long before Gardner entered the scene. Apparently, in 1933, aged seven, young Alec was inducted into a coven by his grandmother, and introduced to the teachings of Crowley, just three years later. However, was this a figment of his imagination created to impress the media and the more subservient members of his covens? In 1961, aged thirty-five, he wrote to Sheffield High Priestess, Patricia Crowther, quite clearly knowing little about witchcraft, and requesting her help. A generous helping of deceit and self-aggrandisement seems to be the norm amongst the hierarchy of the Wiccan movement, although modern witch Yvonne Foley, who knew Sanders, described him to me as an "inoffensive and mild man".

The three covens which were under his control, met regularly on Saddleworth Moor, north east of Manchester. Unfortunately for them, this was the same area where Ian Brady and Myra Hindley buried the pathetic remains of their child murder victims. Books on witchcraft were allegedly found at the murderers' home, and Alec, Maxine and another senior coven member were questioned by the police. Alec and the other man listened to the gruesome tape-recording made by the monstrous duo. Doreen Valiente records that 'Paul' was so horrified and nauseated by it that Maxine refused to listen. Not long afterwards, Alec moved his practices south to London.

Sanders, an open bisexual, claimed to have created a 'spirit baby' with the help of a male witch. He is also one of the few modern witches who admitted to having used black magic to obtain money and sex.

"It worked all right," he told Frank Smyth. But so did the law of opposite and equal reaction. The death of several relatives through cancer, and the suicide of his girlfriend, was the antithesis of his own success. A price had to be paid, and they were the price, he believed. After this he carried out 'ceremonies of purification'.

Most modern witches follow the Gardner/Sanders tradition. But these are the 'young upstarts' of the witchcraft world. Another stream claim to have much older roots, and if correct, truly illustrate a missing link between the witches of 'the burning years' and those of today. They are the 'traditionalists'. Traditionalists claim a continuous and hereditary practice of Wicca from before Gardner. An adventurer called Charles Godfrey Leland met an Italian gypsy witch who in 1897 produced a hand-written manuscript detailing the secret cult of the old religion.

Sanders died in 1988, and although he had originally established his covens along the bleak moors around Manchester, was buried by his former wife, Maxine, in Hastings. One witch I have interviewed who attended the funeral, commented:

"It was a charade. The media were there of course, and so were various assorted weirdos. It was the most Christian, supposedly unchristian, ceremony I have ever attended. There were people playing guitars and singing hymns. But at the reception no-one made a speech or even toasted the man!"

Chapter Four

NOW !

Witches, wizards, ghosties and things that go bump in the night, are enshrined in the whole of European literature, nursery rhymes and folklore learned on Mummy's knee.
Revd Peter Mullen

Now the conflict between Christianity and witchcraft is with us again. The subject is generating heated television debates and raising questions in the House of Commons. Banner headlines cross the front pages of newspapers. Wicca is being classed with Satanism, and associated with the seduction of feeble minds and the physical abuse of children, and even murder. Witches are going underground. The witchfinders in the latter part of the twentieth century are right-wing politicians, Church leaders, television film directors and newspaper reporters. They are as vociferous and single-minded as any of their forebears. You won't see witches hanged or burnt alive, but fire is being fought with fire. One witch present during the public disrobing of a Satanist on live national television commented to me:

"There are a group of people at work here. They are not just in the Churches, but have infiltrated the media. They know how to manipulate public opinion. And they say the camera never lies!"

Who are these people, I asked ?

"The Christian Mafia," she replied coldly.

It has been difficult to persuade many practising witches to talk for this book. They trust no-one. The atmosphere has become heavy with oppression. Six years ago it was a different story. Then the media did not take them seriously. Now there is the pointing finger and accusations of black magic practices, the warping of innocent minds, child abuse and the bloody sacrifice of aborted foetuses.

What is the truth in all this? Do the modern pagans deserve such treatment? If they do, do the ends justify the means?

Chris Bray is the director of a thriving mail order business operating from Leeds, called The Sorcerer's Apprentice. He supplies occult literature, altar candlesticks, horned god incense, hazel magical wands, tarot cards and wax image dolls to thousands of customers across the British Isles and on mainland Europe. Bray would not talk on air to television journalist Roger Cook, but was interviewed by me before the latest troubles. Like others of his ilk he was defensive about his beliefs and sought to present a whiter than white image of Wicca.

"Before Christianity came on the scene, the ancients endowed the environment with the names of their gods. When the early Christian missionaries hit the shores of Celtic Britain, they set about changing these old gods into new devils. That took centuries, and they never did quite succeed in convincing everyone. That's why so many Christian holidays are built around remnants of pagan leftovers.

"There is a quiet revolution going through society, an anti-patriarchal movement of which the Christian movement is the embodiment. Along the pathways of ecology, we are heading towards a softer matriarchal order of things; an attunement with the Earth, the goddess Diana.

"I've got 40,000 customers on my mailing list, but that's only the tip of the iceberg. One witch usually orders things on behalf of several others. I think it's safe to say there must be around 100,000 practising witches in Great Britain today. The vast majority will never leave. People get hooked. They discover it's about a natural energy which can be manipulated for the benefit of all. Witches are less prone to illness than other people, and are more successful in their daily lives.

"Since the repeal of the Witchcraft Act, interest has been on the up and up. Until then, the only people who were allowed to write on the religion were sociologists and Churchmen. Now, books are being published all the time by real witches."

Two such witches who have written several books are Janet and Stuart Farrar. They are High Priestess and High Priest of a coven in Ireland. I watched them a couple of years ago fielding questions from an audience of students during a television debate. Stuart is much older than his wife, but stronger and more confident. Janet is a very attractive lady, but came across as highly strung. I approached them twice while I was researching this book to solicit their comments. I wrote to them through their publishers and then directly to their address in southern Ireland. At the time of writing, I have not received a reply to either letter so their books must speak for them; in particular *The Life and Times of A Modern Witch*. The Farrars make good ambassadors, and their book is an attempt to educate the public into the beliefs and goings on of modern witches. Alas, I found it shallow, and their description of witchcraft practices so squeaky clean it would do justice to a Persil advertisement. It failed to address any of the cult's shortcomings and did not tackle the more extreme and distasteful accusations currently aimed at pagans.

The book is based largely on the answers to a questionnaire circulated amongst European covens by the authors. On Satanism, they point out that the Devil is the Christian anti-God which has been wrongly grafted onto the pagan horned hunting god. One witch, Alawn Tickhill, comments in the book:

> I know a few self-confessed Satanists, and they are all distin-
> guished by their psychoses, which are generally merely inverse
> forms of the same psychoses that afflict Christians.

There is no love lost there. But whether the Devil has horns or not, whether he is the figment of someone's imagination or a real objective entity, Christians draw quotes from the Bible which 'prove' that paganism is Satanism, and like it or not, they are in the majority. So it really is not good enough for witches, who are always available when it comes to promoting a new book, a psychic fair, or some other money-making concern, to bury their heads in the sand when the going gets tough. The accusations have to be tackled. Myth and reality have to be separated. It is in everyone's interest - not least the occultists themselves. The Christian fundamentalists will not let up - they have their God on their side and they have no doubts of the validity of this very strange conflict.

Theologian, Father Francis Marsden, spent six years studying for the priesthood at the Gregorian University in Rome. He was ordained in 1984. He impressed me with his very clear views:

"Witchcraft is a very dangerous area to get into. We're all drawn towards supernatural experiences, which deep down are a desire for God. Unfortunately, people sometimes try to satisfy this instinct in many different ways - some of which are harmful. Perhaps people are turning towards the occult as a reaction against the modern world's neglect of the supernatural. But once you leave the Christian fold, you are at the mercy of demonic spirits, no matter how innocent it appears on the surface.

"According to St Augustine, the Roman gods were an invention of Satan to keep that society in captivity. There is a fundamental difference between 'religion' and 'magic'. As Christians we serve God and place ourselves as His servant to do with as He wishes. In magical practices, the Self is at the centre, drawing power by manipulating spiritual forces. The quest for magic is ultimately selfish, even when supposedly used for good. The ego, rather than God, still sits on the throne. Personally, I'm only sorry the laws against witchcraft were ever repealed !"

The Reverend Peter Mullen, Vicar of Tockwith, Yorkshire, writing in the *Daily Mail* of 9 August 1989, had this to say:

> I was in college, training to be a priest in the late sixties. There was a fashion at the time for debunking all things supernatural. We were hardly encouraged to believe in God, let alone the devil! We were taught that God and His angels had handed over the spiritual care of the human race to an army of enlightened professionals: social workers, sceptical, sophisticated clergymen and the like. The world was ruled by Good - and Evil could be explained away, logically, in terms of deprivation, problems in childhood and difficult relationships.

The Reverend Peter Mullen realised that his training was wrong when he became embroiled in the exorcism of a young boy at the request of his horrified mother.

> In 20 years as a parish priest, I too have become all too used to witchcraft. For the occult is, as I know only too well, positively thriving in modern, high-tech and supposedly sophisticated Britain.

The Church of England currently performs about ten exorcisms a year, after obtaining permission from a bishop and after carrying out psychiatric tests. Canon Dominic Walker, leader of a group of priests and psychiatrists has seen 1,500 cases in the past ten years.

Would the resurrection of the Witchcraft Act put an end to the modern witch cult? Are we really drawn towards supernatural experiences because of a deep desire for God? If that is so, what of those who have abandoned the Christian deity for the god and goddess of the pagan religion? What of them?

Chapter Five

THE MAKING OF A WITCH

'Lilywhite Lilith,
She gonna take you thru' the tunnel of night
Lilywhite Lilith,
She's gonna lead you right.' lyrics by Genesis

Are witches made or born? Are people merely converted to the Wiccan 'religion', or is there an innate desire in them from birth? Above all, is there a common witch 'type' - a model encompassing standard beliefs and utilising universal ceremonial rituals?

A few miles north of Burnley lies Pendle Hill. A haven for sorcery in the Middle Ages, it is still revered today. Below, tucked in the folds of a valley, lies the tiny village of Sabden. It is reached by a narrow road which twists and climbs steeply over the surrounding hills, before plummeting towards the miniature houses below. The terraced cottage where Yvonne Foley lived when I first interviewed her, was easy to find.

Yvonne is a practising witch. An attractive woman with clear blue eyes, I was immediately impressed by her uncluttered attitude to the witchcraft debate, and sincere manner. She smiled and introduced me to her family, then invited me to sit down. The furnishings and decor of the house were so normal. There was no indication at all of what many consider to be Yvonne's eccentric and dangerous practices. Eccentric or not, Yvonne pulls no punches regarding the internal feuding within her own religion.

"Witchcraft is widespread across the country, but a lot of people are in it solely for the exhibitionism. But that's not Wicca - that's 'get me on the telly', 'get me in the newspapers', 'give me my five minutes of glory.' I met one of these in Manchester recently. I knew he was playing about, but he didn't realise he was toying with something which can be dangerous. What he really wanted was for people to tell him how wonderful he is!

"You're born Wiccan, it's not something you can buy through mail order. Even those who turn to it later in life will admit they always felt that way, even as a child. I was Roman Catholic before I turned to the old pagan religion. There's probably about 45,000 genuine witches around the country.

"Things started happening to me around five years old. I knew I was different to other children. I had plenty of playmates, but these were spirit children whom no one else could see. Fortunately, as far as religion was concerned, I was always given a long leash. But my father, a retired army officer, had me educated in a convent. That didn't go down too well with the nuns nor myself!"

Yvonne distils the special powers which seem to surround her into the terms 'clairvoyant' and 'clairaudient'. This means she can tell things about a person's past, present and future by supernormal methods, and receives information by 'hearing' the voices of spirits.

"There is no way the messages I receive are through some sort of telepathy. I know that from experience. The spirits sometimes play tricks on me, and occasionally I am advised by them to turn people away. One twenty-six year-old woman, for example, they informed me was heading for a nervous breakdown, and any information I might give her could have had detrimental effects on her mental well-being."

She started giving 'readings' professionally twenty six years ago, using tarot cards and crystal divination. More recently she decided to adopt a higher public profile, a decision she now has reservations about.

"Until a few years ago I worked at home with a few regular clients. Everything was nice and happy. Then I went on the international circuit. I could write a book about that! It doesn't matter where you are, someone is always getting at someone else. The back-biting is often worse than the absurd theatricals many of them indulge in.

"But I have to admit, that's where the icing on the cake is. I've now over seven hundred clients on my books. I work two days a week at the Psychic Centre in Manchester, and the rest of the time here, sometimes until late at night. By the time I crawl into a hot bath, I'm mentally and physically drained."

Because of the internal cut and thrust within the ranks of the witches, Yvonne keeps this aspect of her life largely private, preferring just to be known as a 'psychic'. But she is Wiccan, and even though there are no obvious signs of this in her house, a back room has been converted into a temple. She agreed to show me inside.

The walls were decorated with posters, photographs and trinkets. Exactly in the centre sat a circular wooden table covered with occult symbols. In the middle of this a crystal ball rested on a piece of dark blue lurex. It was here, in this temple, where Yvonne's clients received their readings.

"I worship the Irish mother goddess, Danu," she explained, smiling. "Every day I carry out little rituals in her honour. Wicca is a natural religion. You don't need juvenile pomp and ceremony."

But doesn't modern witchcraft, as defined by Gerald Gardner and Alec Sanders, rely heavily on complex rituals?

"But all they did was popularise something which was all ready there! They took what they wanted from the pagan religion, and filled it with their own ideas. My faith's purely pagan; Mother Earth, everything which is around you. They delved in the black arts, then went to the white. But other witches could have done more good for the craft..."

She gazed out of the window towards the steep slopes of Pendle Hill. For summer, it was a chill, wet day. Through the drizzle the peak was invisible, swathed in a writhing blanket of dirty white mist.

"The Hill helps me a lot," she whispered, so I had to strain to pick up the words. "I draw a lot of power from it."

Do you belong to a coven, I asked? She came away from the window and her eyes flickered and settled on me again.

"Many years ago I learnt it was better to work alone. Otherwise you end up arguing with people who are on ego trips."

How are you treated by the other villagers?

"You must understand I am not antagonistic towards other people's beliefs. I work with a number of Jews who talk of the coming Messiah, and that's fine by me. I still go along to the local Catholic church, and they come and see me. The Father in the village is smashing. When the missionary priest visited, right away the father brought him up here to meet me. They invited me to mass, so I went and took a bottle of wine. Afterwards, in the vestry, we had a long talk. It was all very nice."

So modern witches do not invite the sort of intimidation their predecessors attracted? Yvonne smiled again, but this time there was bitterness in her expression.

"I know a girl living in North Wales, desperate to move back to Bury. All she did was allow the local newspaper to write an article about her Wiccan beliefs. Since then she is terrified to leave her house. When she steps out to visit the shops, her neighbours stone her.

"There is an old lady in Preston who found half a cat posted through her door. Horrible things happen to witches all the time. It's true they leave me alone, but if I go for a walk in the woods, a sinister interpretation will be put on it. If it was you, you'd just be walking the dog."

I caught up with Yvonne recently in Great Harwood where she now lives after the break-up of her marriage. We started talking about Pendle again and its infamous trials.

"Witchcraft is still very much alive in the area. Why do you think my time at Sabden was so pleasant ? They looked after me there..."

In her new home, Yvonne opened up 'a psychic centre', much to the consternation of her 'witchfinder' neighbour - the Reverend Kevin Logan.

Imagine this: A narrow back road in North Manchester, flanked either side by rows of almost identical pre-war houses. A group of youths idly watch as you drive by, weaving in and out of parked vehicles. Then you see it: a large detached rambling house painted white, Raven's Leach. There is a tree in the front garden, twisted and gnarled, straight from Speilburg's *Poltergeist*. The front door is painted black.

You knock a couple of times, and moments later it is answered by a smart young man in a dark suit. Before you say anything he knows who you are and why you have called. Charmingly, he escorts you into a room to wait.

Outside, July is giving way to August, but here, in this room, a fire roars up the hollow of the huge chimney breast, and a heavy sombre atmosphere drapes over the chaise-longue where you have been invited to sit. An antique cabinet crouches over by the narrow window, and across the room squats another, adorned with candles and a carved wooden mask of Pan - the goat-footed god.

The room is pervaded with the essence of anointing oils, and on the walls hang an eccentric collection of paintings. One in particular draws your attention. A dark brooding landscape on the abyss of storm, it is marred by a tear across the canvas.

Enter Barbara Brandolani.

Barbara Brandolani and Yvonne Foley are as different as chalk and cheese. While Yvonne looks and behaves, at least outwardly, like the girl next door, Barbara is every inch the popular conception of 'the witch'. Yet she is something of a renegade, and thinks of herself as more of a 'magician' than a witch. While Yvonne accepts publicity when it comes along, Barbara, in the past, has openly courted it at almost every opportunity. Yet they are both 'Wiccan' and underneath all the special effects, Barbara Brandolani is just as serious about her beliefs as Yvonne Foley.

Barbara, forty-eight, with very short, blond hair, stands a diminutive five foot one. She wears black tights, a shawl, and heavy black eye shadow.

"Tea, coffee?" She enquires, quickly adding: "But you would prefer a glass of red wine, wouldn't you?"

Barbara Brandolani is already reading my mind.

Her husband, Mario, entered with three glasses and a bottle of Lambrusco. He filled the glasses then retired to a corner of the room, blending with the shadows. Barbara curled up on the black rug at my feet. Her first words echoed those of Yvonne Foley. They had much more in common than one would at first suspect.

"I was brought up as a Roman Catholic, but not because I had to be, but because I chose to be - although I was always drawn towards the mystical religions. I took instructions in the Catholic faith for four to five years. But you can only go so far with Catholicism. If you claim certain experiences during supplications, you are advised by the priest to 'ignore' them. Not always possible. I think there must be a lot of Catholics who have come into contact with the occult and secret sciences, who are too afraid of the consequences to talk about it.

"My father was Irish, but it was my Gran who reared me. She had a bad heart condition. Night after night I remember sitting with her, concentrating on the flame of a candle, tapping its life force, pulling my Gran through another day. All this time I was receiving instructions in the Catholic faith. Other things started to happen to me of which I had little understanding or control. I began writing poems, and what looked like gibberish. Later, experts confirmed it was ancient Hebrew script.

"At this point there was no problem. My new-found powers and Catholicism seemed to complement one another. I thought this gift came from God, you see, but the priest refuted it. He told me I must turn my back on it, burn the poems and embrace Christ. What he didn't seem to realise was that I didn't have any choice. It was there, not of my bidding, but of its own volition.

"In the end I was forced to leave. I wasn't actually told to go, but it amounted to the same thing. The gap grew wider, the hostility increased and that was that. If I'd kept quiet I'd never have experienced what Christians are capable of when they turn on you. After that I became 'Wiccan'."

Barbara Brandolani's conversion from Catholicism to occultism was more traumatic than that of Yvonne Foley's, but the parallels are there. My researches seem to indicate that a number of witches were formerly Roman Catholics. Is there any significance in this, I asked Barbara?

"The Catholic faith, more than any other Christian church, is heavy on ritual. Former Catholics are probably attracted to Wicca for this very same reason. Wicca too, involves a lot of ceremonial 'dressing up' and prayer. A certain type of person must need their beliefs reinforced in this way."

But there are other parallels between these two very different ladies. Like Yvonne, Barbara also has collected her fair share of war wounds from altercations with other witches. One of the things she quickly found was that Wicca was as dogma-ridden as Catholicism. And she is not afraid of saying so.

"I don't care. A lot of them are like 'weekend punks' or 'bedroom sadists'. Dressing up, taking part in naked initiations, sexual intercourse. Playing games. And they're a back-stabbing brood. I don't do anything in the name of anything. There is an anonymous energy which works through me, but I refuse to give it a name, or put a face on it. You won't find me searching the pages of spell books. A process enters my head, and I follow it."

This attitude has earned her many enemies within the Wiccan movement as well as outside it, and even threats to her well-being. But she does not care. She is a very independent lady.

Barbara does not talk about 'covens', but prefers to call them 'groups'. Her 'group' is called The Hermetic Order of the Silver Blade, of which she is High Priestess. It is a 'robed' coven. There is no nudity nor sex. Most members are from middle-class backgrounds. Occasionally, some of the weaker members are weeded out, or in one case, where a member was discovered practising black magic, he was excommunicated. The result of this, the Brandolanis told me, was a series of inexplicable violent acts in their house. For instance, several bird cages were ripped off an inside wall during the night, without anyone hearing a sound.

Things are quieter of late in the Brandolani household. Barbara has become disenchanted with those of her own kind, whom she claims are not prepared to stand up and fight for their beliefs, but are prepared to stand by while she fights their battles for them. On top of that, the centuries-old Raven's Leach is literally crumbling away about her.

Are Witches made or born? Although anyone can turn to the Wiccan faith, it seems that those who may possess genuine psychic powers are born with them. Also, as with the Christian religion, there are very many sects, with their own interpretations of basic beliefs. It is these fundamental beliefs that Christians challenge. To them they are outside the teachings of the Holy Bible. To them they are Satanic.

Chapter Six

THE POWER

I teach you the superman. Man is something to be surpassed.
Friedrich Nietzsche

Do witches really have access to supernormal powers? Indeed, is there such a thing as the 'supernatural', or is the will to believe in such things a catalyst for memory distortion and hallucination? The sceptic who explains away all supernatural phenomena in terms of wish fulfilment and misperception is foolish. The road to knowledge is littered with such narrowmindedness as science has advanced down the centuries. However, what this power will ultimately turn out to be is another matter. Research currently being carried out in the field of quantum mechanics may hold some of the answers. Certainly too many people have experienced the phenomenon, some beyond reproach, for it all to be mass delusion. Occultists in particular claim to be able to 'plug into' this force and manipulate it.

One of the first black witches to 'see the light and tell all' was Doreen Irvine. Born into a deprived background, she ended up on the streets of London where she fell victim to drugs, prostitution, and black witchcraft. This is what she said in a recent interview about her former playmates.

"They have great power and should never be taken lightly. They are able to call up powers of darkness to help them in their evil deeds. They often exhume fresh graves and offer the bodies in sacrifice to Satan. They desecrate churches and holy ground, leaving behind a witch's mark. They are so evil many of them go insane."

Doreen became Queen of the Witches of Europe, and claimed that the more exalted her position in the cult, the greater her own supernatural powers. She described how, in front of witnesses, she was able to levitate several feet off the ground, kill birds in flight by willing them to die, and make objects disappear and re-appear.

On the night she was 'crowned', Doreen walked through a blazing bonfire without suffering any harm. On another occasion, while her coven was carrying out rituals on the moors, they heard a small group of men approaching. The men were journalists and a local vicar. Doreen claims to have made the entire coven invisible to the intruders, who walked past quite oblivious to their presence.

Caitlin Morris is a pseudonym for a BBC reporter who is also on the editorial team of a major national women's magazine. I have spoken to her several times on occasions when our professional paths have crossed, and have no reason to doubt her story.

Caitlin found it impossible to reconcile her busy career with bringing up three young children without the help of a nanny. After the death of her mother, who had been living in a small cottage in the grounds of the house, Caitlin advertised for a live-in child-minder. In reality she was looking for a replacement for her mother; a 'proxy granny', so she knew exactly what she was looking for. Why then did she employ Morag?

The family were inundated with replies, but one phone call in particular was from a woman with a very raw Scottish accent, something Caitlin has an aversion to. As she thought for an excuse to turn the applicant down, she heard herself invite the woman over to meet the children. Even her husband was bemused by this out-of-character decision.

Morag turned out to be small, stocky and sporting fiery red Celtic hair. She was a keen caver and potholer, and before Caitlin realised what was happening she had made arrangements to move in. Morag was a lapsed Catholic, she told Caitlin, who had turned 'to the Old Religion' after a fire had swept through her house, killing one of her children. She said she was a white witch, High Priestess of a coven in the Mendip Hills. She seemed to take great pleasure in telling her employer about the magical power of sexual orgasm, and gradually, Caitlin began feeling intimidated.

As the children were at school, Morag became bored during the day, and said she would quite like the dinner lady's job at the small village school. This was not mere wishful thinking, although Caitlin knew there was no vacancy, and despite the fact that such jobs always went to one of the mothers in the village.

"That is the job I want, and that is the job I will get," Morag boasted. And she did.

She talked to Caitlin about magically 'working on people' and the power of 'retribution', finally admitting she was not a white witch but 'more like a dirty shade of grey.' Morag claimed she was not beyond using The Power to punish people - even unto death. Caitlin decided enough was enough. Even though the nanny had offered no harm to her own family - on the contrary, she seemed to like them - Caitlin realised she could do without this sort of problem. The woman with the fiery red hair went as quickly and mysteriously as she had appeared. All that remained was a notice on the bedroom wall: To will, to dare, to obey, to keep silent. But that was not the end of the matter.

Morag seemed to have left something else behind in the tiny cottage beside those cryptic laws of witchcraft. A friend who came across to help out suffered a terrible night of terror during which she felt a horrible presence in the bedroom. A rector came over and said prayers in the building which temporarily lulled the presence, and the girl was not disturbed for the remainder of her stay. Next came another friend - Ingrid, a children's fiction writer. But the fiction which bubbled out onto the clean white pages in the cottage seemed to be from another hand. As Caitlin explained:

"They all had the same theme - a terrible struggle between darkness and light, good and evil. They were beautifully written, intensely powerful and horrible to read. Each story featured perversions of nature and embodied the demonic side of man."

Eventually the stories burned out of Ingrid's system, but the Power which had apparently imprinted itself on the cottage was far from gone. Caitlin found a permanent nanny, a girl called Sarah, full of vitality and rosy-cheeked - at first. But night after night of terrible nightmares took their toll on the young woman. She became dreadfully pale and lethargic. The final straw came with an early morning dream in which she was bleeding to death. She came out of sleep and was horrified to see thick red blood on the night storage heater. She examined herself - no cut, nothing on her nightie - and looked closely at the stuff on the heater. It was definitely blood. Sarah wiped the gluey mess off then went and told Caitlin. Caitlin decided that something needed to be done. The rector's prayers had subdued the phenomenon but had not stopped it.

Sarah knew a man who had experience in dealing with occult matters. He was invited down and went alone into the cottage. Caitlin described what happened.

"As a psychic with considerable powers of sensitivity he had gone through an horrific time. He would not describe it in detail, but there had been violent manifestations, including objects hurling themselves at him, and suitcases falling off the top of the wardrobe. He found there were actual disturbances in the earth's rhythm, brought about by the misuse of natural energies by Morag's magic. Driving home, John felt extremely ill and had been forced to stop to give himself time to recover."

Caitlin told me that prior to this very strange affair, she had been a sceptic on such matters. Now she has joined the growing band of people who similarly have seen the laws of 'common sense' and science openly flouted and cast aside like empty promises in a politician's speech.

If we are to believe the newspapers, the last witch trial began on 12 December 1983. The place was Livorno, northern Italy, and the accused was a wee Scots lass called Carole Compton. Carole had been working as a nanny after following her Italian boyfriend over from Scotland where he had been employed as a waiter at the Turnberry Hotel. The relationship had ended, but the girl had decided to stay on in view of the poor job prospects back home. This proved to be a terrible personal decision.

Carole worked in three different houses. But strange inexplicable things happened in these places. A picture of the Madonna fell from a wall, objects mysteriously moved about, a key turned by itself in a lock and a water heater had gone berserk when the girl was nearby. But worst of all were the fires.

There were five in all. The second caused £5,000 worth of damage, and the final one almost effected the death of a three year-old child when her mattress started burning. The police were called and the apparently bemused twenty year-old was arrested. Carole spent fourteen months awaiting trial in deplorable conditions forced to co-habit with drug addicts and prostitutes. All that time she stuck to her story of absolute innocence, and yet the coincidence between Carole and the fires was too much. There had to be a link.

How had Carole been branded a 'witch'? Serena Macbeth, a television documentary film-maker who was on holiday at the time of the arrest, offered herself as an interpreter to Carole's Italian solicitor, Sergio Minervini and his assistant, Scottish advocate Lawrence Nisbet. This is what she had to say:

"Minervini told me it had all started as a joke. While discussing the case with Nisbet he had remarked: 'Scotland's full of witches isn't it ?' Then at a press conference, Nisbet told reporters that Carole was 'on trial for witchcraft'. It spread like wild fire, and soon all the papers were filled with this nonsense about 'the witchcraft trial'. Minervini was very embarrassed."

Despite what some newspapers told their readers, Ms Compton was not on trial for 'witchcraft', but faced one charge of the attempted murder of little Agnese Cecchini and four charges of arson. But one could have been forgiven for thinking so considering the medieval motifs of the trial. Carole was escorted into the courtroom by armed soldiers then locked inside a steel cage. A number of foreign journalists interpreted this to mean that the authorities were afraid of her. Actually the cage had been constructed five years earlier for Red Brigade terrorists and had never been removed.

On the third day, attention was drawn to an old woman wearing black, muttering in the gallery. To everyone's amazement, she shuffled towards Carole, holding high a large wooden crucifix. Before she could be restrained, she managed to pour 'holy water' over Pamela Compton, the girl's mother. Her name was Ciara Lobina, a well-known clairvoyant and faith healer. Apparently the Devil had come to her in a dream with knowledge that both women were possessed by the spirit of a young eighteenth-century witch who had 'given them the power of fire.'

Actually there is no proof whatsoever that Carole Compton had any links with Wicca, or indeed even knew anything about the subject. What is interesting given that this happened as recently as 1983, is how Carole's alleged powers were interpreted in terms of witchcraft, especially, it seems, because they had the potential for great harm, and in the case of little Agnese Cecchini, serious injury and death. But what about the fires? There lies a real mystery.

Carole was never seen acting suspiciously or caught near the scene of the fires, in fact to the contrary, she was usually well away when they were discovered. No spent matches were found, and it was scientifically verified that no inflammable substances were used. These fires did not seem natural. They burned in a pattern which could not be repeated in scientific tests.

A fire officer from Bolzano who had examined the sites of three of the fires, told Serena Macbeth, who was now involved in making a documentary about the case, that one of them had exhibited the ferocity of a fire which had been burning for hours - not minutes. He noted the peculiarity of flames which burned downwards.

In court, Professor Vitolo Nicolo of Pisa University, added: "In all my forty five years of this kind of investigation I have never seen fires like this before. They were created by an intense source of heat, but not by a naked flame."

20/20 Vision, the company Serena Macbeth worked for, asked Dr Keith Borer, a British forensics expert, to conduct tests of his own. Afterwards Borer admitted he was stumped. In the worst incident, a wooden stool where the fire had started, was virtually untouched while the rest of the room was destroyed. Seemingly, at one point, the fire had 'jumped' a couple of feet lower, and sideways into a drawer.

Yet even though all this evidence was presented to the court, it was not even considered. Dr Hugh Pincott, founder of the Association for the Scientific Study of Anomalous Phenomena, (ASSAP), headed an international team of parapsychologists who put together a dossier for use by Ms Compton's defence lawyers. It contained many case histories of spontaneous fires which had broken out in conjunction with other poltergeist phenomena, such as that described at the Compton trial. Such phenomena, it is thought, emanates from people who are not in control of it. This can often be a young woman.

But the supernatural ace was not played, and the court were left with just two conflicting facts: There was no evidence at all to connect Carole with any of the fires, yet she was in the vicinity when every one of them started. This was too much for coincidence.

The trial lasted five days. The jury were out for six and a half hours. At the end of it Carole Compton was found guilty of two charges of arson and one of attempted fire-raising. The attempted murder charge was dropped. Carole was given a two and a half year prison sentence, but was released immediately because of the time already spent in prison. The Italian authorities were happy to see her go. The case had caused them much international embarrassment.

I spoke recently with a journalist who met Carole and her mother when they arrived back in Britain. He accompanied them back home to Scotland. Even that was not plain sailing.

"We were quite amazed in view of all that had happened," he said, "when the car engine blew up!"

One of the questions which cropped up time and again during my investigations, was whether or not demons had an objective existence. Are there really evil entities who can slip from one dimension into another, sometimes at the behest of black witches, or is it down to vivid imagination coloured by drugs and alcohol ? One of the best examples is the succubus and incubus - demon lovers of mortal men and women. This phenomenon is more wide-spread than popularly believed. I corresponded only recently with a lady who was having these experiences:

"I wanted to tell you about certain strange things that have happened to me. One thing I am really frightened of at present is that I have 'something' in my house. A friend has told me that this thing is called an 'incubus'. When the 'thing' comes, I also have an experience of leaving my own body at times. The whole thing is weird and I really don't know what I can do to stop it.

"These strange things started around 1985 or 1986. Since mid 1986, I have had 'the visit' from the incubus. It is not just in my bedroom but in other parts of the house too. It never hurts me or marks me but I can assure you I am not some sort of CRANK. Both myself and my family have had strange things happen, but I have never known anything as bad as this. I really am frightened in many ways and I can assure you that I am neither dreaming or imagining these things."

One of the most convincing cases I have come across is that of psychologist and medium Stan Gooch. In his highly articulate book *Creatures from Inner Space*, Gooch describes the arrival of his own demon lover:

I was lying in bed in the early morning, awake but drowsy, with daylight already broken. I became aware of another person in bed with me. For a moment I totally dismissed the idea. Then she - it was a she - moved a little closer, pressing me more urgently. With a sense of rising excitement, which I tried to control, I somehow knew this was a 'psychic entity'. I knew it was not a real person who had got into my room by normal means.

I tried to let the entity go on controlling the situation, but my own interest was naturally very intense. Without opening my eyes, I realised that the 'person' in bed with me - in front of me, was a composite of various girls I had once known including my ex-wife, but with other elements, not drawn from my memories in any sense. In short, this entity, though possessing physical and even psychological attributes familiar to me, was none the less essentially its own independent self. It was not solely compounded of my imagination - or, at least, not entirely of elements which I consciously recognised. It was its own creature, but seemed, as it were, to be using part of my own experience in order to present itself to me.

On this first occasion my conscious interest in the situation got the better of me, and the succubus gradually faded away. On subsequent occasions, however, the presence of the entity was maintained, until finally we actually made love. From some points of view the sex is actually more satisfying than that with a real woman. For my own part, like the heroes of many folk tales and fairy stories, I am more than happy to settle for a relationship with a succubus, and the world of real women (but what does 'real' mean?) can go whistle.

Stan Gooch has combined his professional work and personal experiences to explain the phenomena of the poltergeist, spontaneous fires and demons - a power which the witch claims can be tapped for good or ill. While he believes that these phenomena are real, he has also concluded they emanate from the human mind - a belief also of many modern 'chaos magicians'. The seat of this creation, the unconscious mind, is located in the cerebellum. There resides an infinite number of sub-personalities and psychic energies. These can be released by accident or by design. In the case of demons, once released, there is a possibility they are able to take on an independent existence of their own. Tibetan mystics have maintained this for centuries.

Looking back, hysteria did not explain away all of the powers allegedly released by the witches. At Salem, for instance, many things were reported that today would be termed poltergeist manifestations.

In 1682, a meeting of prominent Quakers was persistently troubled by a stone-throwing poltergeist which smashed crockery. Father and son, Increase and Cotton Mathers, who played prominent roles in Salem during the witchcraft trials, were often at the centre of supernatural phenomena. One remarkable case was that of Margaret Rule. She, like many other young women, went into fits, as if she was oppressed and possessed by invisible powers. In one instance, witnesses observed 'something' disturb the girl's pillow, a distance from her. One of the Mathers made a grab and felt a creature not unlike a rat between his fingers before it escaped. This phenomenon repeated itself at other times. But by far the most impressive event was when the afflicted girl levitated towards the ceiling of her bedroom, as she did on several occasions. Those present tried violently to bring her down, but to no avail, until she came back down of her own accord. At least eight of the observers signed sworn affidavits to this effect.

And what of the belief that witches can fly ? Perhaps they can, in a fashion. Today there are hundreds of documented cases of people who claim they can leave the body at will and float around, travelling some distance. These 'out of body' experiences are prevalent too with people near death - a phenomenon currently being intensively and scientifically investigated.

It seems plain that The Power spoken about by witches is more widespread than commonly recognised. Labels are an invention of the conscious mind. The power to move objects, cure people of incurable ills, bring them harm, conjure up demons - seems more than mere delusion. If this power truly emanates from the inner space of the unconscious mind - could it be the real forbidden fruit?

Chapter Seven

The Witchfinders
The Reverend Kevin Logan

You shall not permit a sorceress to live. Whoever lies with a beast shall be put to death. Whoever sacrifices to any god, save to the LORD only, shall be utterly destroyed. Exodus 22

In Britain today, the witchfinders have returned. In the dying embers of this century they do not have the unconditional backing of state bureaucrats - although that is being sought in Parliament. Nor do they favour an armoury of physical tortures, burnings and hangings in their battle with 'occult forces'. Nevertheless, it is the same old war, with the same old battle cries and the same old adversaries.

Today's witchfinders are skilled communicators and know how to utilise the media to their best advantage, indeed some of them work in the media. The tabloid press which titillated its readers until a few years ago with stories of eccentric business-men and bored housewives taking part in witch orgies, now feed an audience brought up on hack-horror paperbacks and video nasties, with lurid claims of ritual rape and child sacrifice. Whether the aim is to excite or horrify, the result is always assured - high viewing figures and volume newspaper sales. But do today's Christian witchfinders get their message across in a society which, some may argue, is no longer overtly Christian ?

The Reverend Kevin Logan is on the forefront of what he believes is a battle with the Devil. A former Roman Catholic and journalist, he has appeared in many television documentaries and live debates on witchcraft, and published a book, *Paganism And The Occult*. Logan is softly spoken, and was honest in his replies to my searching questions.

I motored over the Lancashire moors one bright warm day to Great Harwood, where Kevin Logan is Vicar of St John's. Ironically, this is the place where the child Alec Sanders spent the war years, escaping from Hitler's military and occult madness. The gate to the Vicarage was cradled in summer growth from the abundant garden. During our interview rock music hammered down the stair well to the front room which serves as a study. Framed behind glass on top of a bureau stood a copy of the cover illustration from his book. The inscription beneath the circle of ancient standing stones said it had been presented by his publishers. I commented on the nice gesture, but Logan faltered in his agreement, in case enthusiasm inferred vanity, I presumed. Perhaps that was the reason it had not been hung on the wall.

"We are surrounded here by about thirty witches' covens," he began, pouring coffee. "I was at a secondary school yesterday speaking about witchcraft, because Wicca exists in the school. In another local school, a coven is quite active and the kids are having trouble because of it. They're scared, they're losing their bearings, they're dabbling in things they don't know. Some of the kids are active participants and they are being encouraged by outsiders."

I nodded, but for the moment I was more interested in the man himself. How long had he been a reporter, and what made him make the change from Catholicism to the Church of England? I was especially interested in his answer to this latter, as several witches I had interviewed started out as Catholics.

"I was brought up on Roman Catholicism which taught that you lived a good life and built up credits by going to mass and helping old ladies across the road. At the end of your life you spent a thousand years suffering in purgatory while your fate was decided. God totted up all the good points and all the bad points. If the good outweighed the bad then you went to Heaven; if the bad outweighed the good, and you were really black with mortal sin, you went to Hell.

"Now, anything to do with sex was a mortal sin! As a seventeen year-old with healthy desires, and keen eye sight for a pretty girl, I was obviously destined to go to Hell... I became pretty sick of God. He was always threatening to drop me into the fires of Hell. I stopped going to church and concentrated on journalism instead. I was in that for twelve years and worked for various weekly papers, including the *Lancashire Evening Telegraph* and a public relations magazine for the NCB.

"Then when I reached twenty eight I hit a low period in my life. Nothing was going right; my personal life was in tatters. I began asking the questions all over again. What's it all about? I began to reach out for God. Instead of listening to what churches told me, I read the scriptures and discovered a completely different God. I found a God who loved me. He sent his son, Jesus, to die on the cross at Calvary to pay the penalty for my sins. This God didn't make threats. Instead He offered me the gift of eternal life; the gift of His friendship and love. I said; Yes, I want to know more about you, and invite you into my home. My life underwent a tremendous change. Different personal relationships, different ideas, a different purpose in life, a new job, an intimacy with this God in Jesus."

A lot of pagans I've spoken to, I interjected, turned to the old religion because they didn't like the way the Church was run.

"I fully sympathise, I wasn't enamoured myself. But their bad experiences were of Churchianity, and not of Christianity."

But they would argue, I continued, playing Devil's advocate, that Christianity has abused its position down the centuries, and is still doing so. In Lebanon, in Northern Ireland where two Christian factions are at war with one another - where even clergymen take an active role in aiding terrorist murderers. Things like that don't give Christianity a good press, do they ?

The Reverend Logan hunched up and looked down at the carpet before replying in his slow precise way.

"It is a case of man taking something over which is intrinsically good and beautiful and twisting it to his own ends. How many husbands do that with sex? Sex is the most beautiful and perfect way of expressing one's love for one's wife, but we've turned it into something which is horrific. We abuse children with it, rape old women, use it for trading for favours or money. Man has abused Christianity in that same way. Especially when power, money and state have become involved. When politics takes a hand religion is crushed. That's why Christianity was dead for a thousand years up until the Reformation.

"From the conversion of Constantine everyone jumped on the Christian bandwagon. The Church existed - not in the Vatican; that was just a corruption, a rotten stinking empty facade - but in the outbacks of some of the monasteries. Christianity is a personal relationship with Jesus and has nothing to do with Northern Ireland. In Northern Ireland, men are nakedly using their own denomination, their own hatred, to justify their own cry for justice.

"If I took that line, I would demand the return of the ducking stool. I would be launching a witch hunt. But I speak to these witches and my heart goes out to them. I know they're lost. They put a brave face on it, and tell me how marvellous their lives are, but I see the emptiness in their eyes. And I see their families who have been torn apart because of their beliefs."

The Reverend Logan takes a very active part in undoing the damage he alleges has been caused to people through their involvement with the occult. He is part of a team of 'Deliverance Ministers'.

"The Deliverance Ministry applies the power of God to cast out evil spirits who have taken control of a person's mind and body or are affecting them in some other way. We could be talking about possession, oppression or simply obsession."

It sounded like a low key version of *The Exorcist*.

"Yes, but I think we've run away from the term 'exorcism' these days. 'Deliverance' sounds more sensitive in the light of Hollywood, and exorcisms which have gone wrong."

Indeed, there are exorcisms carried out by Christian ministers which have gone disastrously wrong. The worst example is the case of Michael Taylor who, it was claimed, was possessed by forty demons. Taylor obviously had chronic psychological problems before he and his wife, Christine, became involved in the Anglican Fellowship at Barnsley, Yorkshire. It was there that they met Marie Robinson, who became a regular visitor to their home. Taylor became obsessed with the twenty two year-old, and on one occasion kissed her. But Marie rejected his advances, and he fell upon her, driving her into a corner, poised for attack like a wild beast. Marie was convinced she was a whisker away from being killed. It was only the fact she kept repeating the name of 'Jesus' which averted murder, she later claimed. Taylor was convinced that Marie was possessed with an evil spirit which had tried to seduce him. In the months to come, critics would claim that Marie, far from being a lay preacher, was in reality a witch, because of her obsession with the full moon.

Taylor later told police Marie was to blame for what subsequently happened:

"It was that woman. The evil came upon me after that. We had a battle of wills. She seduced me with her eyes. I can still see those eyes. I saw her standing naked before me and I was naked. She was looking at the sun. She turned and her eyes became slits and I felt the evil within me. But I fought it, oh how I fought it, but it overcame me."

After the attack on Ms Robinson, the Anglican Fellowship agreed to exorcise the thirty one year-old man. The all-night ritual took place at St Thomas' Church, Gawber, Barnsley, on 5

October 1974. Present were the Reverend Peter Vincent, Reverend Raymond Smith and their wives, Mr Donald James, a Methodist lay preacher, and a Mr John Eggins. Christine Taylor remained in the vicarage next door.

The exorcism took place in the church vestry. Taylor lay on a pile of hassocks arranged cross-like on the floor. Around him the exorcism team sang songs and said prayers, demanding that the demons leave his body. At 7am, 6 October, it came to a close, although neither the exorcists nor Taylor felt the conclusion was satisfactory. Taylor was to tell police:

"They tried to bring me peace of mind, but instead they filled me with the Devil."

The Reverend Vincent commented that he had seen the look of murder in the man's eyes after the ceremony. One of the helpers there said:

"I have the word from the Lord that the spirit of murder is going to break out."

They pleaded with Mrs Taylor not to go home with her husband, but she would not be parted, and was convinced that Jesus would protect her. She went - and she died.

A neighbour described hearing a noise, then seeing Taylor outside, naked except for socks, his hands, face and body covered in blood. Inside was the fresh corpse of his wife, her tongue and eyes torn out. He had ripped her apart with his bare hands.

Michael Taylor was found not guilty of murder at Leeds Crown Court, because of insanity, and sent to Broadmoor - a top British hospital for the criminally insane.

At the inquest, those involved in the exorcism came in for severe criticism, particularly the Reverend Peter Vincent, for allowing Christine to go home unprotected. Even the Archbishop of Canterbury, Dr Donald Coggan, admitted the affair was a shambles whilst maintaining the right of the Church to carry out exorcism where psychiatry had failed. Some of the most damning comments came from psychiatrist, Dr Hugo Milne, who had examined Taylor in Broadmoor. Dr Milne said that at the time of the murder, Taylor had been in a trance, insane. He said:

"When people talk of spirits leaving the body, it is in fact a physiological condition caused by rapid breathing, leading to aggressive and uncontrolled behaviour."

What did Kevin Logan think of 'demons'? Do they really have an independent existence, or are they purely subjective, a product of the mind?

"I must admit I leaned towards the psychological, the subconscious for an awful long time. I became a Christian and I still wasn't convinced of the reality of the Devil and evil spirits. I had to wait to experience that side myself."

The watershed experience came one New Year's Eve with a phone call from a desperate father. Apparently his son had become mixed up with a group of Satanists and was terrorising his family. Kevin Logan visited the house without delay and talked to the parents about their normally introverted, slightly built son. He had acted as front man for the group during various escapades, and had twice been arrested by the police and sent to Risley Remand Centre, near Warrington, a place notorious for its suicide hangings. Psychiatric reports had given the boy a clean bill of mental health. Logan was also able to ascertain that in this instance neither drink nor drugs had played a part. Yet there he was, at the top of the stairs wrapped in a grubby bed sheet, making theatrical ghost noises. The vicar was suddenly convinced that here was no psychological phenomenon, but genuine demonic possession.

"In the name of Christ, and with all His mighty authority, I command you to leave that boy", he cried. The youth gave out a scream, threw off the sheet and ran into his bedroom. They ran up after the boy and noticed that a green-reddish glow permeated the room. The boy was nowhere to be seen. Reverend Logan repeated the command, and on the third occasion the boy's heavy single bed rose violently into the air and slammed against the ceiling. The slim youth appeared from beneath it, and with an inhuman roar, flew at his mother, his thin boney fingers clamping around her neck, pushing her back over the landing rail. Logan, a heavily built man, tried to prise them apart, and was flung violently aside with the mother. The boy ran into a second bedroom, almost wrenching the door from its hinges.

They found him dazed, his eyes clearing, the diabolical snarling replaced by a frightened whimper, a young boy emerging out of the clutches of the Satanical monster which had apparently possessed him. He came round to find the vicar astride his chest, and no memory of the four hours of terror that had been visited on his parents.

"The people I have tried to help have left me with a deep conviction they are in the grip of powers which are not simply a demonstration of mental illness, it's something else entirely. Something that has a grip on them, something that with prayer can be broken. I have seen time and time again the power of prayer and the victory of Christ."

But I wanted to know more about the objective reality or otherwise of these alleged 'powers'.

Occultists claim they can conjure up various supernatural entities, but I wondered, if I was standing outside the room looking in through a window, would I also see what they were seeing ? Can demons be ordered or brought into our world ?

"Yes, I'm convinced of that. But some of those who do it aren't convinced of it's objective reality. They conjure these things up in a triangle while they stay protected in a circle. They can conjure up any particular thing they want depending on the ritual. But they may say it's something created from their own minds. That it isn't reality as we understand the concept. I would want to say to them they are *wrong*. Not only is it reality, it is of an evil nature. It's not simply a product of their imagination.

"God is real *and so is the Devil*. One of the difficulties about witchcraft is that the terms 'objective' and 'subjective' are meaningless bases. Reality is turned on its head. What we see, what we feel, that is reality. Reality is what's inside. So it's rather like turning the world inside out, like wearing a shirt with all the seams on the outside. They say we see the world with the seams on the outside. That makes it extremely difficult, because they then make up their own rules."

But aren't they just putting themselves at risk, and if so, shouldn't they be left to get on with it ?

"They're hurting themselves and dragging others into it. One of the great concerns we have now is that it is hitting the High Street in an evangelical way. They've got shops and mail order outlets. There's one they're trying to open in Hynburn, and another in Bolton. Already they have the cinema and video industry doing a marvellous propaganda campaign."

I knew from personal experience the truth of that. My brother's business is in video film hire. I was glancing over his choice of videos and asked if he had any 'quality' films. I couldn't see any.

"My customers don't want anything like *that*," he replied. "They want horror, and the more violent and scary the better."

Even so, surely people are capable of telling fact from fantasy and right from wrong ?

"For those brought up against a stable family background there isn't much of a problem. As far as Christian homes are concerned you're not too susceptible. Unfortunately, there's not enough of these... For many people reality is shaped by television, and that reality is warped. Allied with that you have to appreciate that many people's lives aren't all that pleasant. So if there's a susceptibility, or weakness, to fantasise then we've got problems."

It was not so much a case of the Devil finds work for idle hands, as, the Devil finds work for malleable minds.

"Take the case of Michael Ryan. He received instructions to kill 'the terrans' in an occult fantasy game. He was told: You wake up in a forest. There is a throbbing in your head, a madness...Your gun is in your hand, you know what to do... Five weeks later he walked into Savernake Forest and killed the first of sixteen Hungerford victims.

"The New York Times reported on a sixteen year-old who was jailed for murdering a younger boy. David Ventiquattro was addicted to the computer fantasy game Dungeons and Dragons. The game required that he had to 'extinguish evil', and he became convinced that Martin Howland was evil and had to be killed."

Kevin Logan cited many more cases of murder and mutilation where the aggressors had a link with witchcraft and the occult. In some instances the link was strong, in others tenuous. Without denying that a minority of people are motivated to psychotic behaviour through involvement with occult paraphernalia, several things occurred to me when studying these reports.

Millions of people play occult video games, read horror and fantasy novels, and watch black magic films. But they keep it all in perspective - it is just a piece of scary fun, entertainment. No doubt the vast majority involved in occultism are not into grossly indecent sexual behaviour and child sacrifice. So I wonder about the tiny minority who do go over the top and might commit atrocities.

The Reverend Kevin Logan commented that the cases he discusses are those where mental illness has not been diagnosed and where the courts have treated the culprits as normal criminals. That may be so, but I have yet to meet two psychiatrists who agree about anything. Psychiatric evaluation is not like painting by numbers. There are no hard and fast rules. So much of it comes down to personal, albeit, professional, opinion. There are other pressures, too. If a criminal is diagnosed as 'psychotic' then he will be charged with manslaughter, and not murder. Manslaughter carries a much lighter sentence, and who wants to see a convicted child killer back on the streets?

Michael Ryan, in common with other mass killers and rapists not linked with the occult, was a 'loner'. A social outcast who sought revenge on a club which he perceived would not offer him admittance. As Ryan shot himself before the mental health specialists could get at him, we have no way of knowing whether the psychopath was lurking in the recesses of his subconscious waiting to be triggered; or whether the cause of his actions was a flirtation with the occult.

I think it's fair to say in these extreme cases that the aggressor was already a psychopath and perhaps their occult involvement served as the trigger; otherwise the whole world would be in a state of total anarchy. One witch has argued with me that if someone searches deep enough they might discover that all these people also shared an interest in chess, yet no-one would suggest that chess was 'Satanic'. There have been cases too, where convicted killers have claimed they were driven to the crime by the voice of 'God'. Religious mania of any complexion is a dangerous and uncontrollable thing.

Perhaps, if evil does exist as an independent intelligence, then it can take advantage of individuals already psychologically flawed, and push them to do things the rest of us could not do even if the Devil and his hordes had their claws in us.

Witches become very upset when the press links their religion with Satanism, so I asked Kevin Logan where he thought the dividing line lay between Wicca and Satanism.

"That's one of the real problems, nobody knows. Witchcraft branches off into Satanism, chaos magic, occult magic, up into the psychic and the paranormal. These people don't know what they're into at all. Some of them follow old manuscripts, or the writings of Aleister Crowley, Gerald Gardner, Austin Spare or study shamanism. Maybe they're Alexandrian or Dianic witches. But they all speak with different tongues. They refer to the force they try to manipulate as 'Brama', the 'mindforce', the 'cosmic energy', the 'cosmic masters' - in witchcraft there are so many names it would take all afternoon to list them. Who is telling the truth? How can occultists go around selling it to other people when they don't know what it is they are selling? There's no foundation stone. Nothing to stand on. Just empty space. It's all guess work, delusion and fantasy. But they will argue their case black and blue. I just smile on the sidelines.

"They cannot defend themselves when I talk to them. They don't know the truth of their own case. There's no documentary evidence. In Christianity, at the very least I can go back two thousand years. There was a Jesus Christ, there was a crucifixion, and there are reports by historians that His grave was empty, that He rose from the dead..."

But people have argued with that, I said.

"Yes, they have. But with the number of manuscripts we now have, it is far superior in its documentation to even Julius Caesar, and no-one doubts he existed! I can give a dozen good reasons why there is a God, based on sound philosophical and theosophical arguments. When witches talk it's all guessology. How intelligent professional people can be taken in by it is one of the wonders of the world!"

I leaned forward earnestly on my chair.

If it's all airy fairy superstition, then why are Christians so concerned in smashing it ?

"Because of the damage it's doing to susceptible people, because of the evil force which is behind it."

"But what of the likes of Yvonne Foley and Janet and Stuart Farrar ? They claim to simply worship the Natural forces which bind the Earth together. They seem to have more in common with the Green Party than Satanism."

"I've spoken to Yvonne Foley on the telephone, and she comes across as a charming lady. But let's not fool ourselves with talk of white witchcraft and black witchcraft. I think that most respectable occultists will acknowledge there's no difference between black and white magic - there's just 'magic'. There is power. And it's up to the individual how it's used. There's no such thing as black and white magic, but there are black and white people. They will use the power for good or bad; for healing or for cursing."

Reverend Kevin Logan feels he has had his fair share of curses thrown at him. In fact he advises fellow Christians not to allow pagans to take photographs of them, in case they are later used as a focus for psychic attack. One witch whom he claims laid a curse on him was Steve Raven, real name Paythornethwaite, whom Logan refers to in his book as 'the dwarf'. The confrontation occurred when local churches were planning to erect a twenty foot high rolled-steel cross on Pendle Hill. Apart from its strong witchcraft connections, Pendle was the place where George Fox experienced visions which were instrumental in him starting the Quaker movement in the 1640s. Nevertheless, the local witches viewed the enterprise as desecration of their holy ground.

The national media carried the story, and the *Burnley And Padiham Mail* with the headline; PROBE INTO WITCH 'WAR', had this to say in their edition of 29 October 1987:

Reports that Christians plan to throw a 'ring of prayer' around Pendle Hill on Hallowe'en were being probed by police. Church-goers are said to be organising secret prayer meetings on the hill to combat Devil worshippers. But as hundreds prepare to make their traditional pilgrimage on Saturday night, police said they would be making inquiries 'from a safety point of view.'

Great Harwood Anglican clergyman Kevin Logan refused to comment on the national newspaper claims in which he was named. But he said:

"On Hallowe'en we are dealing with spiritual warfare."

The Evangelical Alliance, with over a million followers nation-wide, were reported to be behind the hillside gathering.

"Thirty covens throughout East Lancashire will be initiating members on Hallowe'en," said Mr Logan.'

In his book. Kevin Logan added:

The Witch who had given me the warning about the cross - a barrel-chested dwarf balancing in his elevated boots - stood at the time on the pathway of my vicarage and looked up at me in defiance. He played nervously with his assorted occult jewellery and then pronounced a curse on our home and work.

Paythornethwaite was not afraid of speaking his mind, and made these comments in an article published in the *Lancashire Evening Telegraph* of Wednesday 26 November 1986.

"Christians have ruled the roost for a long time. But today people are better educated and they know the damage that Christianity has done. It has destroyed civilisations all over the world, created untold misery and death. Now it is dying out. Today people want a religion that offers personal freedom, that is ecologically viable. Wicca teaches respect for animals and the Earth, and protection of the environment."

The cross never was erected; the local council would not grant planning permission. But Kevin Logan records a more tragic ending for the Darwin witch:

"Several months later he was dead. He had suffered a fatal asthmatic attack aboard a plane en route to an international magic convention in Mexico."

Despite their differences, Kevin Logan says he had taken a liking to the twenty nine year-old man, enjoying the challenge of their theological sparring, hoping one day to bring him back to Christianity.

"It's a shame about the way he died. And I really shouldn't have said 'dwarf'."

But was Paythornethwaite right? is Wicca popular because of its ecological message, and are woman attracted to it because of its softer matriarchal image, in the 'Earth Mother'? 'God' is perceived as being masculine, and the Christian Church has always been controlled by men. Even in this enlightened age, the Church is still firmly in the hands of men, with women taking a secondary role. The demand by some Christian women that they should be allowed to take positions in the Church hierarchy on a level with men is currently causing a split in the Church of England.

"This sort of thinking stems from two problems. Firstly, men have abused their privilege, their status in the Church. Second is the reaction of women over the last thirty years. It's no wonder there's now a great move to make God into a woman! The Earth Mother concept is tailor-made. Many feminists are turning towards Wicca, towards nature religions. But in Christianity, God is both male and female; and man and woman were made in that image."

Yes, but according to Genesis, the first woman was made from Adam's rib. Because they were not both created at the same time that makes women sound second-class.

"That's right. Man was created first, women to be help-mates. But throughout scripture, women are given the same status as men, but they serve a different function. The Bible acknowledges that men and women are different, and that man's role is to lead. A woman has no trouble obeying her husband, if her husband is loving his wife as much as Christ loved the Church. Man is described as head of the family - but not in a dictatorial sense. It's a partnership. But the husband's the senior partner."

This sounded like Orwell's cynical comment from *Animal Farm* that "all animals are equal, but some are more equal than others".

Kevin Logan's thorough knowledge of occult matters has raised a few suspicions from time to time amongst witches and members of his congregation that he might not be all he seems. I was reminded of the Reverend John Lowe, described in Chapter Two, who was offered up as a witch by his parishioners and subsequently hanged.

"One witch said that as I know so much about the subject I must be a witch myself ! That's ludicrous. My knowledge of witchcraft comes simply from asking questions and listening. There was one lady in the parish who wasn't sure I should be allowed to baptise her child. I said come and listen to me in church, and after three months, if you still think I'm a witch we'll have a talk."

Tragedy door-stepped St John's Vicarage on the night of Thursday 15 February 1990. It was on that evening that a former Satanist, Caroline Dawn Marchant, known as 'Hannah', killed herself in the house.

sister of Sarah M. ? ↓

The *Lancashire Evening Telegraph* later told the story in a front page article written by Perry Gourley and Lynn Ashwell. DEATH WISH OF DEVIL GIRL said:

> A young woman given sanctuary by a vicar after a life of satanic worship took a fatal over-dose at his home, it was revealed today.
>
> And the tragic girl's solicitor has called for a second post-mortem examination to be carried out on the body "to look for satanic markings or signs that she had given birth."
>
> The solicitor, who did not wish to be named for fear of reprisals, denied that the Rev Kevin Logan had exorcised the girl. The Liverpool-based solicitor said Caroline had become involved in a Satanist group after being blackmailed over photographs taken at a teenage party.
>
> She eventually escaped from the group and changed her name to try to stop the Satanists tracking her down.
>
> "We're talking about people who do some horrible things to others," he said. "They are taught that the only escape is death."
>
> But the sinister group desperately wanted her back, he said.
>
> "The Satanists believed that she had certain power. The girl was under tremendous pressure."
>
> Caroline was due to meet the solicitor to give detailed confessions about what she had been involved in with the group.

The death had deeply affected Kevin Logan. The twenty three year-old girl, born in West Drayton, Middlesex, had met the vicar at a Christian conference in Brighton just a few days before.

"Hannah Marchant had no home to go to, so my wife and I decided that she could come and stay for a while at our vicarage. We tried to welcome her and make her feel at home. We knew that she was suffering from depression and that she had tried to commit suicide twice in the previous three days. There were three main things troubling her.

"First, Hannah was afraid that a large network of Satanists with whom she had been involved would find and kill her. She had been caught up in some of their Satanic crimes, including child abuse and child sacrifice, and she had decided that she would see a solicitor and make a complete confession. She knew this would involve naming names. She had made the decision to do this even though she feared the consequences.

"Secondly, she had left the Satanists and become Christian some time before this decision. She knew that the Lord had forgiven her, but she had found great difficulty in forgiving herself. She kept saying she could not stand the screams of the children in her head. She also had a seven year-old boy who was still with the Satanists and she could not stand to think of what was happening to him.

"Thirdly, Hannah had lived with a caring family in the South for nearly two years but had made their life so difficult that they could no longer cope.

"When she woke up at our vicarage with all this and other things crowding into her poor mind, it was evident that she felt she could not cope any longer. Unknown to us, she had brought with her a large bottle of drugs prescribed by her doctor. She swallowed the contents, about seventy pills in all, and then wrote out a suicide note.

"In the note she said that she hoped to escape Satanism. She was sorry for destroying people's lives and asked for their forgiveness. She prayed that Jesus would accept her. Hannah gave the note to one of our house guests who immediately passed it on to me. I took Hannah in my car to Blackburn Royal Infirmary, arriving mid-morning."

'Hannah' quickly deteriorated and was admitted to the intensive care unit. She hung on until Monday 5 March, where she passed quietly away in the early hours.

The inquest, which was held on 7 March, recorded an 'open verdict'. The inquiry itself caused some controversy. The *Lancashire Evening Telegraph* complained that neither the press nor the Reverend Kevin Logan had been informed of the investigation. Actually the newspaper had been told, but mysteriously, a few hours before the hearing, a man who claimed he was the Coroner's Officer, telephoned to say it had been cancelled. This may or may not have had anything to do with a feud between the Coroner and the newspaper.

When I spoke to Kevin Logan about this, he had the impression that coroners had the authority to turn a 'public' inquest into a private affair if they thought it was right to do so. But not according to the *Lancashire Evening Telegraph*:

'Rule 17 of the Coroners' Rules states that every inquest shall be held in public, save that an inquest or part of an inquest may be held *in camera* in the interests of national security.'

In any event, only two people were present at the inquiry; Coroner George Graham and his officer, Police Constable Clive Carroll.

In the newspaper report, the solicitor, Marshall Ronald, who Hannah had planned to 'confess' to, had called for a second post-mortem. I asked Kevin Logan if this had been granted.

"Yes, it was. The examination revealed marks consistent with what Hannah had described in her diary. And there was evidence that seemed to show she had given birth at some time. Although there is no official record of any birth."

The vicar also revealed to me that in her belongings was a partly written manuscript detailing her experiences. In which case, I asked, has there been a police investigation, will there be arrests, and has her son been found ?

No, there were not any names, or details of the whereabouts of her son, he told me. I found it hard to believe that the girl had not left some sort of statement which would allow the authorities to track down these alleged child murderers, and lock them away - especially with the involvement of her own flesh and blood. Kevin Logan did not see it that way.

"When a person is planning suicide they don't think or act rationally."

The girl's diary, letters and manuscript were given to Blackburn CID by her father, Mr Les Marchant, and later passed on to the police in Wiltshire. But without names and addresses, it is hard to see what can be done. This lack of facts, as will be seen later, seems to be a feature of the child sacrifice controversy. Yet it is being used to fuel the witchcraft conflict.

Investigative journalists David Hebditch and Nick Anning produced a long article on the case for *The Independent on Sunday* published on 30 December 1990. In it they claim that their investigations showed that Caroline Marchant's story of involvement with Satanists was just that - a piece of fiction. They tracked down former school friends, foster parents and room-mates who all said they had never seen any evidence or indication that Caroline had either become pregnant or been involved in Satanism.

Michael Green, the Leeds pathologist who carried out the second autopsy, conceded that his judgement had been influenced by Marshall Ronald. According to Hebditch and Anning, he now withdrew his original findings and observed that "pathology is like a computer. If you put garbage in, you get garbage out."

Indeed, the journalists seem to have found a prosaic explanation for the scars which Caroline had claimed were inflicted on her during Satanic rituals. Caroline was placed into care after the divorce of her parents and lived in various institutions, sharing a room for a time with another girl called Sarah Cloughessie. Sarah described how Caroline had her forearms and hands bandaged after she had continually scratched herself, drawing blood. Sarah often begged her to stop. The wounds would go septic. She did this all over her body, and told her room-mate that on one occasion she had placed a knife in her vagina.

Hebditch and Anning's investigation seems to show that claims of Satanism only emerged after Caroline had become involved with Christian fundamentalists. Clearly she was a very disturbed young woman who was worried about being rejected by her new 'family'. Was the story created to make the bonding more secure?

Reverend Logan believes, however, that such stories do illustrate the growing strength of Satanism and black witchcraft.

"I don't acknowledge there is a neutral Power. There are forces like electricity, but they have to be generated. When you go back to the beginning of the world and its origins, I have to say there is a first cause, there is a master designer, there is a super intelligence, there is a God. One God, one Power, one Force. Yes, God delegated power to Lucifer, his right-hand man. But Lucifer tried to wrest the universe, the world, from God. He failed, *but Lucifer is still here, and he's still got that power*."

Chapter Eight

The Witchfinders
Geoffrey Dickens MP JP

And where the offence is let the great axe fall.
William Shakespeare

Geoffrey Dickens has generated hundreds of news headlines in the eleven years since he started alerting the nation to a shadowy secret world where young children were physically, mentally and sexually abused by family friends, neighbours, and, even more disturbingly, their own parents. 'Incest', a taboo word even amongst police officers and some social workers, had been allowed to flourish behind closed doors and curtained windows. This social myopia allowed bruises to go unseen and nightmares to be interpreted in the light of television programmes and fantasy comic books, rather than real bestial assault. Ironically, the testimony of children sent many hundreds of innocent people to the stake and the gallows three centuries ago. Is this why stories told by children have been ignored since? A case of 'cry wolf'? Children like attention. Children tell fairy tales. But children do get ill-treated, and sometimes they die. The difficulty is in separating fact from fantasy.

Child abuse was suddenly an open debate, not just here, but in the United States too. The British media threw their heart and soul into it, and the subject peaked with the Cleveland scandal. In Cleveland, 121 children were diagnosed as having been sexually abused in the first half of 1987. Dr Marietta Higgs and

Dr Geoffrey Wyatt were later suspended for being over-zealous. But the paediatricians, in an interview for *The Observer* on Sunday 29 April 1990, were unrepentant. They believe that the real numbers of child abuse cases have still not emerged because of disbelief. But critics compared tests used by these doctors with the witch-prickers of long ago. Little did anyone realise that this was the direction the child abuse phenomenon was destined to go.

On 15 April 1988, the national media reported on a press conference with Mr Geoffrey Dickens, Conservative Member of Parliament for Littleborough and Saddleworth. He claimed that many people had been convicted of offences against children carried out during witchcraft initiation ceremonies, and demanded a debate on the subject in the House of Commons. The debate took place, albeit a brief one; an adjournment debate, on 28 April of that year. His fellow MPs were far from convinced when Dickens told them that witchcraft 'was sweeping the country.' In fact some of them saw fit to joke about the matter. Dennis Skinner suggested Dickens was right; witchcraft was here, in Downing Street.

According to Hansard, Geoffrey Dickens said in part:

"This black magic influence is so strong and dangerous that the power and command over adults and children is total. Disgusting ceremonies are held, in which children are sexually abused by Satanists. Paedophiles are joining such groups because they have found yet another way to get their hands on children whom they know will be too terrified to talk."

The MP was after resurrecting the Witchcraft Act abolished in June 1951.

Most 'white' witches refused to believe that child abuse occurred in connection with witchcraft practices. However, Doreen Valiente, in *The Rebirth of Witchcraft*, makes this comment:

"I wish I could say, as some Witches and occultists have said, that such allegations are all nonsense. Unfortunately, I have press cuttings which bear out Mr Dickens' statements to the letter."

John Patten, Minister of State for the Home Office, replied to his colleague's speech by pointing out that existing laws already covered child abuse and the desecration of graveyards. He also made the following statement:

"It is a basic tenet of an open society such as ours that a person must be free to hold the beliefs that he or she wishes, as I am sure that my honourable friend agrees, but that principle is certainly modified by a clear requirement that any acts arising from such beliefs must be within the bounds of the criminal law, and I know that I have my honourable friend's agreement on that point."

I have corresponded with Geoffrey Dickens on the matter of his involvement with the witchcraft debate, and although he was unable to make himself available for interview, did send me some material together with an enthusiastic covering letter. Over the past two years he has taken part in many live radio debates and has been interviewed extensively by the press and television. The following dialogue is in fact a compilation of his replies to the questions put to him by several interviewers.

In a way it seems natural that Geoffrey Dickens should carry out a crusade on behalf of children, and involve himself with the witchcraft question. His constituency covers an area infamous for the diabolical torturing and murder of several children by Myra Hindley and Ian Brady in the 1960s. The moorland towns and villages round about his home are steeped in witchcraft history and today have a concentration of covens.

Nevertheless, his critics claim he only involved himself in the child abuse campaign for the publicity it would generate in furtherance of his political career. This latest twist in the tale is seen by some as vindication. Mr Dickens deftly side steps the allegation:

"That could be said, of course, but for the ten years I've spoken out on this subject we've seen some dramatic changes. We've seen announcements that it will be illegal for anyone to possess child pornography. There are new arrangements so that evidence from children in court will be treated more sensitively via a video link. We've also seen 'leave of appeal' against too lean a sentence in such cases. So the things I've spoken out against have forced the law to change for the benefit of children everywhere."

Mr Dickens has been quoted as saying he would like to 'wipe witches off the face of the Earth.' Witch, Barbara Brandolani consulted the National Council for Civil Liberties about this remark, and they said, according to her, this could be construed as stirring up hatred towards a minority group.

"I don't think abolition is obtainable! I realise now we'll never get legislation in the House of Commons outlawing witchcraft. Certainly there is no danger of witches being dunked in the village pond or burnt at the stake. But I think we can legislate to stop any person under twenty one being enticed or recruited into secret occult groups. I think that would have the approval of many parents, because it would mean their children would have more maturity of mind, and could see more clearly what they're getting into.

"It does frighten me that children are taken into these groups from a very young age. They get so frightened by what they see and what they hear, they become psychiatric cases. If it was down to me I would ban witchcraft, I don't agree with what they're doing. But it's not down to me."

Many witches have argued that they do not allow children near their covens. This is what Mrs Brandolani said.

"I'm really confused. I find it incredulous this thing to do with children. I've never considered allowing children in. Children have never approached me at all - ever. I think Mr Dickens is talking about people initiating their own children. Well, I don't even approve of that! I think he's making a massive generalisation."

It has been argued that Geoffrey Dickens is using the child abuse issue to tarnish the Craft in the style of Matthew Hopkins. One set of statistics indicated that four out of five cases of abuse occurred in the family. Does this corrupt the Christian view of the family, asked Barbara Brandolani ?

"You are trying to take a minority group and make it the cess pit for any wrongs in society. Well it won't wash - you can't do that, you can't make that sort of generalisation. Your attitude allows anyone going before a court tomorrow to plead; the Devil made me do it."

But Dickens was unrepentant:

" My attacks have been on people who practice black witchcraft and Satanism. White witches make a great play of telling me the difference between them and black witches. White witches are part of the pagan religion and wouldn't harm anyone, I'm told. Yet one of them appeared on television holding my effigy, and said if I became too menacing towards her cult she would drive a steel needle through it and bring all sorts of bad things down on me.

"They can't have it both ways. They're either one or the other. But it's a very complex subject, and growth is tremendous, with shops springing up all over the UK. I'm very worried about the activities of Astonishing Books and Sorcerer's Apprentice in Leeds. Librarians tell me there's always a queue for books on black magic. We have graves all over the country which have been desecrated. Coffins opened, heads cut off, fingers severed. This must be very distressing for the bereaved. Those now serving prison sentences have said quite clearly that it is part of black magic ceremonies.

"We've had surveys of young children. In one recent survey of 300 thirteen year-olds, 87% admitted they'd dabbled in the occult. I thought it was about time someone spoke out and said to parents; be careful, don't let your children dabble in witch-craft, be it white, black, or any other colour."

I have heard of other similar surveys and wonder on the reliability and interpretation of such statistics. Exactly what is meant by 'dabbling in the occult'? If a child has played the board game Dungeons and Dragons, watched a horror video or read a Stephen King novel - does this mean he has 'dabbled in the occult'? Some Christian fundamentalists are even arguing that horoscopes in the daily newspapers should be banned.

But what about the charge that he is 'picking' on Wicca because of his own Christian beliefs?

"Not true. This was· new to me. I hadn't realised that paedophiles had found another way to get their hands on children, then put the power of the Devil into their minds. This gives the paedophiles tremendous power over them. Not only can they then do as they wish, but these children are absolutely terrified of telling anyone of what's happening."

On Tuesday 8 August 1989, the *Western Mail*, along with many national newspapers, published the story of Peter McKenzie, under the headline: FIFTEEN YEARS FOR WIZARD WHO HAD SEX SPELL.

Self-styled wizard Peter McKenzie lured school-girls into his "magic circle" by promising they could become witches if they obeyed his orders - and the first was to have sex with him.

The 38-year-old salesman recruited 13 girls, some as young as six, giving each a special witchcraft wand to Asmodeus, god of lechery and debauchery.

McKenzie, a bachelor, had sex with a number of the girls and carried out depraved acts with the others. They were all forced to take an oath of secrecy. But finally one of the "magic circle" broke the spell when she blurted out to her mother, "I've got a secret."

McKenzie, of Hemel Hempstead, admitted 24 offences - four of rape, four of attempted rape, 12 of indecent assault and four of unlawful sexual intercourse.

Judge Kenneth Machin jailed him for 15 years, saying, "No one sitting in this court could be other than totally horrified and nauseated by your conduct perpetrated over a number of years. They are quite frightening and terrifying offences. It has done incalculable damage to the emotional development of several of the children."

On 9 August 1990, the *Daily Mirror* reported on the case of 'evil satanist' Reg Harris who was jailed for thirty months at Worcester Crown Court for using two under-age teenage girls as 'sex slaves'. According to the report, the sixty five year-old man rigged his house with fake magical effects to bring the girls under his power. He made them listen to a tape of the Devil, recorded by himself, and told them he could destroy them by burning their photograph. He tape-recorded their sex sessions, and when they finally broke free he set fire to their home.

Geoffrey Dickens continued:

"I must say I've been consistent all the way through this. When I found that ministers in the Church of England were dabbling with children, I went to see the Archbishop of Canterbury to ask him to sort out some of his vicars."

Abuse by the clergy is an ongoing problem too. In one of my local newspapers, *The Journal* of 17 August 1989, appeared a story headlined: CHURCH MAN MOLESTED GIRL. It told how a recruitment officer for The Church of God had indecently assaulted a school girl who attended one of its Sunday schools. The thirty three year-old man admitted at Bolton Crown Court four offences of indecent assault when the girl was eleven and twelve. He was jailed for eighteen months. The Church of God is a Christain fundamentalist organisation.

But Dickens is convinced that 'Satanic' abuse goes further than sexual molestation.

"I managed to get a former witch to concede, on live television, that babies had actually been sacrificed. Six hundred children go missing every year. At least fifty of these children are never found. How can this be? People don't disappear into thin air. Murder is horrible enough to contemplate, but in most cases of this nature the child's pitiful body is eventually discovered. With witchcraft sacrifice nothing is ever found. I checked with the Home Office and even they do not keep reliable records of missing children. It's a difficult and tricky area to prove."

One of Geoffrey Dickens' arguments against the occult community is that it is a 'secret society', the innuendo being that anything 'secret' must harbour illegal and immoral activities. Freemasonry has come in for similar criticism. Witches have argued with him that Wicca is not a secretive religion, but he asks, if that is the case, why do witches adopt occult names?

Barbara Brandolani:

"It started during the burnings. People were afraid of being found out. Now it's partly tradition, but many of us are still afraid of persecution. And your comments are fostering this persecution!"

Many people have come forward to claim miraculous cures brought about by occult healers when conventional doctors have failed them. Barbara Brandolani herself believes she helped her son who was born with an incurable disease, by working with a force from within herself. Does Mr Dickens think that psychic powers actually exist?

"Many Christians go to church when they have someone in the family desperately ill, and pray to God that they will recover, and of course many of them do. I don't know whether or not I believe in 'psychic powers'. But there was an old boy in a village near Padiham who was able to cure warts on childrens' hands by just touching them. In a fortnight they would completely disappear. There was such a great belief in his powers that the village schoolteacher sent any child with warts to see him. Apparently this thing had been passed down through his family.

"Look, I don't care what people believe in. If they want to believe they've got psychic powers, fine. Although it is a kind of vanity. When you profess to have such powers it is vanity. Wiccans can practice whatever they like, but when paedophilia, orgies and other things take place which I totally disapprove of, they've got to expect Christians to be quite disturbed. Where you have shops selling books on witchcraft and black magic, and contact magazines the alarm bells start ringing.

"It becomes menacing, it becomes a threat, it is something we must try to limit. I don't think people quite realise the scale of it. There are some terrible groups coming across from America to the United Kingdom. It's the spread, it's the scale of the operation, it's the businesses building up, it's the alarm bells which are ringing...That's the worry."

That might be the worry, but what are the facts? For months Mr Dickens had told the media of a dossier of cases which had been sent to the Home Secretary. When this was checked out, however, the Home Office made this statement in a letter dated 7 March 1989.

> According to press reports, Mr Geoffrey Dickens MP has sent the Home Secretary a dossier of child abuse cases allegedly connected with witchcraft. However, this has not been received and the Home Office has no other evidence that there is a problem of the kind Mr Dickens describes. The Government is satisfied that the existing law on child abuse would be sufficient to deal with any offence against children which might be connected with witchcraft.

Chapter Nine

SACRIFICED

"Astaroth, Asmodeus, princes of affection, I conjure you to accept the sacrifice which I present to you, of this child, for the things which I demand of you..." Words spoken at a black mass in seventeenth-century France

The Gloucestershire country town of Wotton under Edge has in its midst an historical and archaeological gem. Yet it was due solely to the determination of one man, that it was not lost forever beneath the planning inspectors designs and the crushing caterpillar tracks of the bulldozers.

The Ram Inn was built in 1189, and over the intervening eight hundred years very little has been done to change its basic structure. On the contrary, when John Humphries bought the building in 1968, it was in a dilapidated state. He learned from a local newspaper that Whitbread had put it on the market at £3,500. John felt immediately drawn towards the medieval relic and managed to convince the brewery that it was only worth £2,500! Recently, an executive from that same brewery called by and shook his head in wonder that his company could ever have let it go.

Not long after John moved in, however, he learned that the local council had put a compulsory purchase order on the property. They wanted to knock it down to widen the road! John started a hard and lonely campaign to defeat the Town Hall

101

bureaucrats. He approached, amongst others, the Historic Build-ings Council for financial aid and support in his fight. He received neither. It was his own determination plus the will of the local people which forced the council to back down.

With just train driver's wages and a few extra pounds earned through bed and breakfast, John set about making the run-down building habitable. He tore off the corrugated roof that some uncaring philistine had nailed to the ancient rafters of the adjoining barn and began researching the Inn's history.

The old place became an obsession. Holidays were a thing of the past. John's marriage broke up, and he lost touch with his daughter for fifteen years.

Renovation has been limited due to lack of time and financial constraints, but during the course of the work he has learnt many new skills, impressing professional builders who have visited. In a way, that has been a good thing for the Ram. Extensive renovation tends to rip the heart out of a building. This relic of the past still possesses an essential primitiveness. BBC pro-gramme-makers must have felt the same uniqueness when they used the Inn for location shots during filming of the historical drama series, *Poldark*, in the late 1970s.

The Ram Inn, John discovered, has a very colourful past. He uncovered a priest's hole and a bricked up tunnel which once led to the church opposite. Two of England's last highwaymen hid out in the Inn, and the building was notorious for several murders. Perhaps this explains the Ram's plethora of alleged hauntings... Although I experienced nothing supernatural during my short stay, apart from a sudden drop in temperature, John showed me and several colleagues bundles of letters from guests who had sighted apparitions, and experienced poltergeist activity.

The church was built a hundred years after the Inn, the carpenters and stonemasons lodging in the older building while the other was being erected. There is even a memorial to Stephen

Hopkins, a local man, who sailed with the pilgrim fathers on the *Mayflower* in 1620.

John Humphries dug deeper into the past, and discovered that the Norman foundations were set in bloodied earth. It was during excavation work in one of the rooms that the grave was discovered.

A local dowser told him there were bodies buried beneath the foundations. John dug up the floor of one of the rooms with the help of a local archaeologist, and recovered the bones of several children along with two broken ceremonial daggers. At about that time John also discovered an ancient Saxon map which clearly showed that both the Inn and the church were built within a circle bounded by other buildings and the surrounding streets. Close by are a number of steps carved into the side of the hill. At one time these terraces were used by monks for the cultivation of vines, although they are much older than that. These too were a feature of pagan times, especially in Egypt, where much of the modern witchcraft beliefs and rituals come from. Height is connected with spiritual superiority. The soul of the departed king or shaman would rise up the staircase to a higher plane. Steps were also a feature of pagan sacrificial altars. God banned the Jews from using steps in Exodus 20.26.

This perfect circle is still evident on a modern map of Wotton under Edge. A ley line also passes through the Ram adding to its magical significance. John Humphries believes that the area within that circle was an ancient pagan sacrificial site, and the victims were children.

That was not unusual. From the eighth century BC to the Roman destruction of the city of Carthage in 146 BC, thousands of urns were recently discovered containing the calcined bones of small children, sacrificed by fire. There is ample evidence in the Hebrew scriptures that at one time the ancient Israelites sacrificed their first-born. The story of Abraham, Genesis 22, is a graphic example. In these verses, Abraham's faith is tested when God orders him to take his son, Isaac, and sacrifice him.

> When they came to the place of which God had told him, Abraham built an altar there, and laid the wood in order, and bound Isaac his son, and laid him on the altar, upon the wood. Them Abraham put forth his hand, and took the knife to slay his son. But the angel of the LORD called to him from heaven, and said, "Abraham, Abraham !" And he said, "Here am I." He said, "Do not lay your hand on the lad or do anything to him; for now I know that you fear God, seeing you have not withheld your son, your only son, from me." And Abraham lifted up his eyes and looked, and behold, behind him was a ram, caught in a thicket by his horns; and Abraham went and took the ram, and offered it up as a burnt offering instead of his son.

Does this biblical account have a direct connection with the Inn and the unholy ground it was grafted onto? Child sacrifice/ the Ram Inn? Coincidence, or that most intriguing of Jungian concepts; synchronicity ?

Child sacrifice, as we have seen, has a strong historical precedent. More recently, what is claimed to be the largest sacrificial site discovered in Europe was unearthed near Peterborough, according to *The Independent* of 24 June 1989. It consists of a nine hundred yard sacred avenue and artificial island constructed from an estimated two million timbers. Ritually deposited swords, daggers and jewellery was found alongside the remains of animal and human sacrifices. As in the case of those found at the Ram, the weapons had been ritually broken in half.

Most of the material found so far dates back to the Bronze Age - 950-850 BC; but according to Christian fundamentalists, human sacrifice is still going on, and has been continuing for centuries within black witch covens, and Satanist Temples. In particular, one former witch has stated on television and in newspapers that she witnessed some of these ceremonies. On the ITV programme, *The Time, The Place*, broadcast on 1 December

1988, a former black witch, Audrey Harper, made these statements:

"I experienced black witchcraft in the early sixties, although I didn't know what I was getting involved in. I was invited to parties where I was introduced to coven members who met once a month. At my initiation ceremony I was raped on the altar then I witnessed the sacrifice of a child. It was a baby which had been born to someone in the coven, and was therefore unregistered. But it wasn't just babies, they sacrificed older children, too."

When asked why she has not reported this to the police, she replied:

"The police wouldn't believe me. All they were interested in was that I had been raped. As a member of the coven we were taught to recruit. We started with thirteen year-olds. They were very susceptible at that age, and mixing sex and drugs meant they were hooked onto something which was very exciting. The experience cost me nearly a quarter of my life in mental hospitals. God set me free."

In the *Daily Star* of 3 June 1988, is a front page story headlined: HUMAN SACRIFICE. Inside is a follow-up titled: DAY I SAW SATAN KILLING. There is a photograph alongside the text which shows a blond-haired woman in witchcraft regalia. This, we are told 'is Marion Unsworth before she renounced Satan.' The feature states in part:

A young virgin died a horrible death as a human sacrifice in a deserted churchyard. The thirteen year-old girl, wearing only a cloak and a mask made from birds' wings, was led to the altar - a flat tombstone. Then the high priest of a Satanist coven plunged a sacrificial dagger into the girl's breast - and the midnight ritual slaughter was over.

The bloody scene was witnessed by mother of three Marion Unsworth, who was a high priestess of Britain's occult covens for twenty years.

"It was appalling," said Marion, now a devout Christian. "It was a very heady atmosphere, with a lot to drink - but I'm convinced I saw that child being killed."

She claims the human sacrifice took place in a West Country graveyard in the late 1970s.

Before her conversion to Christianity, Marion was a regular in the Sunday newspapers during the 1970s for black magic practices. In those days she was notorious for enrolling two of her children into the cult as well as generating headlines such as WITCH CURSES HER MUGGERS.. A LOVE CURSE LED TO DEATH PLOT..THE BLACK WITCH RIDING ON A VROOMSTICK..HALLOWE'EN BOY GETS GRUESOME BIRTHDAY..TERROR WITCH'S BISHOP WAS ON A DEATH LIST..

She took great delight in telling the *Sunday People* of 15 May 1977, of how successful her curses were:

In one type of death curse you have to go through a funeral ceremony in a churchyard. You make a little doll in the image of the person you want to die, put it in a little coffin and bury it - with a photograph of the person if possible. You do it when the moon is fading.

Another method we use is to make a wax image. We burn it slowly and as the doll burns, the life of the person it represents slowly fades away. We burn it at coven meetings once a week or month and they get sicker and wither away.

Surrey Constabulary investigated Audrey Harper's claims in December 1988, but the results of that investigation were not made public. One wonders if Chris Anderson and John Mahoney, the authors of this article, approached the police to check Marion Unsworth out ? Unsubstantiated claims of murder should not be used as an excuse for entertainment.

Another Audrey Harper sound-alike, 'Anna Dixon', was interviewed in *Chat* magazine during February 1988, and Harper herself appeared in that bastion of journalistic truth, the *Sunday*

Sport for 13 March. *SHE* magazine for 21 September published as part of a long feature the by-now familiar allegations of an unnamed former black witch:

> I was a black witch for five years, and for the next seventeen I was in and out of mental institutions and had extensive ECT. During my time as a black witch I saw and did things that I shall never be able to forget. The coven I joined initially got me when I was heavily hooked on drugs. They supplied my heroin free, so, of course I could never have backed out even had I wanted to.
>
> Covens have always actively recruited kids, the younger the better. But now it is getting worse. Their methods have become bolder, their ways more devious. What happens typically is this: some kids are asked if they want to come along to a party on Saturday night. They get there and it all looks ordinary. The party begins and the kids are relaxed. There are hypnotic flickering candles. They feel drowsy but they are enjoying themselves. The candles have been heavily injected with an hallucinogenic drug. Within half an hour they can, and will, do anthing they're told. Clothes are thrown off and the children manipulated into sexual acts.

According to the report, these activities are photographed to blackmail children into keeping quiet and force them to become full members of the coven. The confession continues:

> Initiation ceremonies can take many forms. You never know what your's will be. Mine was to be violently raped across the altar by the High Priest. Others can be 'tested' by various ordeals. I once saw a thirteen year old girl raped in a similar manner.

She also commented on her involvement in human sacrifice:

> Once, it was a baby girl, nine days old. She belonged to a woman in the coven. Her throat was cut. We drank the blood.

Audrey Harper was interviewed a few days after *The Time, The Place* in the *The Post* morning newspaper, and in the *Western Daily Press* on 17 May 1989.

There are some obnoxious people on the periphery of occult-ism. However, is it significant that these stories have been largely picked up by the tabloid press, and ignored by the more serious newspapers? Is it not disturbing that prominent Christians should allow themselves to be interviewed by the *Sunday Sport*, a newspaper fundamentally based on soft porn and the mockery of deformities in human beings? Or is it a case of the ends justifying the means?

I cannot understand journalists who publish extreme and repugnant allegations on the word of one person without attempt-ing to find substantial proof - or if that proof is lacking, saying so to put that person's claims in perspective. Unfortunately, most newspaper editors and television directors will not let a lack of facts stop a good story from going out. Is that why the heavy press initially ignored the issue, because none of these allegations could be proven?

Unless people are arrested, charged and found guilty in a court of law, we do not know whether the claims of ritual murder and rape made by Audrey Harper happened or not. She must know the people concerned, but so far no police action has been taken. At her own admission, Harper spent seventeen years in and out of mental institutions. What reliability can anyone place on someone's recall when they were drugged up, boozed up and then spent the next seventeen years having their mind unscrambled?

Harper published a book on her claims which received an uncritical review in the March 1991 issue of *Direction*, the magazine of the Elim Pentecostal Churches. In *Dance with the Devil*, she asks "Why, oh why won't the authorities believe these horror stories? It's as if there is some official plan to refuse to acknowledge the existence of Satan. Yet child abuse seems to be on the increase everywhere."

There have been other stories in the press of child sacrifice. Self-confessed Satanist, Derry Mainwaring Knight, was jailed in 1986 for seven years on charges of fraud. It was claimed he conned several wealthy Christians out of £250,000 to finance a covert crusade against other Satanists. His victims included the Reverend John Baker, Michael Warren JP, Lord Hampden, Lord Brentford and Susan Sainsbury - wife of Tory minister Tim Sainsbury.

During his trial, which generated national headlines, Knight said he was a 'Grand Archdeacon of Satanism' and 'High Priest' of a temple which carried out black masses in Hockley Wood, Essex.

It all started when Knight approached the Anglican vicar, a kindly if naive man, in his parish at Newick in Sussex, begging for financial and spiritual help. He claimed he was a reformed character who knew a way of destroying his former colleagues. In fact, all he did was rip everyone off, living the life of Riley, buying expensive cars and running a high-class prostitution racket.

From her American hideout, a former mistress of Knight's, Angela Murdoch, said her lover had bragged of abducting three children who were sacrificed during Satanic rituals. The only evidence she saw of this was a jar of blood she found in the refrigerator.

Was this just juvenile bravado designed to impress his girlfriend? Certainly the police never picked up on this aspect of the case - a familiar state of affairs. My attempts to speak to the prisoner in 1987 were mysteriously blocked by HM Prison Service. Was Derry Knight really a Satanist? Plenty of influential Christians thought so.

During the trial, the Reverend John Baker never gave up on the confidence trickster. He believed all along that Knight had the power to put curses on people, and during visits to his prison cell begged him to refrain. John Baker died in February 1988 of leukaemia.

One case of human foetal sacrifice which was to have gone to court was allegedly dropped by the Crown Prosecution Service because the young girl involved would be unable to stand the strain of a lengthy trial, according to the *Sunday Mirror*, of 21

May 1989. It quoted Detective Inspector Charles Horn, who led the investigation:

"In all my eighteen years in the Force, I had never heard a story like it. But I believe this girl. I am convinced she was telling the truth."

The 'truth' was that the girl claimed she was one of a stable of 'brood mares', women procurred for ritual intercourse, after which the aborted foetus was used during black mass ceremonies. She had evidently been introduced into the cult when she was just eleven by her grandmother. The grandmother and five men were at one stage arrested and charged with procuring an abortion and rape. A statement by the Crown Prosecution Service seems to set out clearer the reason why the case was dropped:

> Because of the nature of the evidence by the principal witness, we considered that it would be unsafe and unsatisfactory to put before a jury.

In other words, it was her word against theirs.

Latest of these claims emerged in August 1990, when a twenty six year-old women, hidden behind a screen in a television studio, claimed she was lured into a coven by her grandfather at four years old. There, over the next twenty two years, she was gang-raped and claimed that babies were being sacrificed. A major article about the allegations appeared in the *Manchester Evening News* on 10 August. The woman, known as 'Sarah', was apparently recovering from her ordeal at Rochdale's Birch Hill Hospital. Rochdale was to become a national talking point over the next few months.

Sarah told of coven members drinking blood and urine, smearing their bodies with excrement and eating human remains. She claimed she had been forced to take part in perverted sex, and had been kept in cages and boxes with snakes and insects. Although she has never actually witnessed child sacrifice, she does claim to have heard screams. As the victims were aborted foetuses one wonders how this was possible. One sacrificial murder was observed however. This involved driving stakes through a member's body who had 'transgressed'.

Time and again we have read scenarios that seem to have more in common with Dennis Wheatley and horror videos than reality. But a pattern was already emerging that threatened to tip the scales away from subjectivity towards a more objective interpretation. That pattern was one of social workers and some other professionals lending their voices to a belief that bestiality and human sacrifice were a way of life for alleged victims of black witchcraft. We have no way of knowing whether or not these professional opinions have been coloured by religious conviction.

Sarah's champion was psychiatrist, Dr Victor Harris, consultant at Birch Hill Hospital. He claims that a police surgeon who examined Sarah confirmed that she had been subjected to multiple rape. This was backed up by journalist Matt Finnegan, author of the article, who told me he had heard it from a police officer working on the case. Harris is convinced that the woman is telling the truth. He compares her clinical symptoms with those exhibited by victims of Nazi atrocities:

"This woman is not crazy or prone to invent things. Her psychological reaction to abuse, torture and experiences beyond the norm are identical to those of victims of the concentration camps. She would have had to do an awful amount of research in psychological textbooks and be an accomplished actress to make it up. She has also provided the most mundane details about these rituals and covens, which a liar would not bother with. In my professional judgement she is telling the truth."

Dr Harris and Sarah, heavily disguised, appeared in the BBC television series *Close Up North*, on a programme called *Beyond Belief?* transmitted on 4 October 1990.

I found Harris less convincing on camera than on paper. The programme began with the psychiatrist filmed in profile, chain smoking. When he was interviewed, you could see the pain in his face, hear the sincerity in his voice. Perhaps there was too much pain, too much sincerity. Matt Finnegan told me that Harris had convinced a lot of people, including some police officers. He added:

"The officers were certain that Sarah was telling the truth, in the sense that she believed it."

During the programme, Dr Harris admitted he had known Sarah prior to her admittance at Birch Hill Hospital.

We also learned that Sarah was still allegedly being abducted for Satanic purposes. The arrival of a car to the house would follow a telephone call from a member of the sect. Sarah would be forced to lie down behind the front seat on journeys to secret locations, where she would sometimes remain for four days at a time. Her abduction is made possible, we were told, by brainwashing techniques used on her as a child. Amazingly, neither her husband, friends or neighbours realised what was happening. According to Sarah, her husband only found out about her bizarre double life when he came across her diary.

According to her, the sect uses a variety of locations, including the cellar of a disused warehouse. This latter was the size of a large hall, decked out in black satin with wall to wall carpeting, and equipped with all the implements and regalia expected of a black witch coven.

When the programme interviewer put it to Sarah that the police required evidence in order to carry out prosecutions, she admitted:

"It's not going to be stopped unless they are caught in the act. I couldn't help them because of the repercussions. I would be too frightened."

I would imagine that the headscarf and disguised voice would not fool her life-long abductors for more than thirty seconds. If these Satanists really do exist, then her life is already in danger. What does she have to lose in naming names and providing evidence to the police? They have already committed child sacrifice and the murder of one of their own. Dr Harris supports her claims that in Rochdale alone there are fifty members of the sect, and even more in Manchester.

A week before transmission, a Manchester witch was contacted by a BBC researcher on the programme. He wanted to send a film crew to record her practising various occult rituals. This footage was for inclusion in the *Beyond Belief?* programme. She says the BBC did not tell her that the programme was to include claims of ritual rape and child sacrifice! Fortunately, this lady turned them down. If the filming had gone ahead, viewers might have assumed that she was directly involved in the atrocities being described by Dr Harris, Sarah and the BBC. Were the programme-makers so desperate for 'evidence'?

It is all too reminiscent of the witch trials of the Middle Ages, where those caught up in the hysteria created the most outlandish and hellish scenarios, spurred on by officials from the Church. Yet a simple psychological explanation might not suffice to explain this phenomenon.

In the *Sunday Mirror* article, Maureen Davies, described as a Church social worker, commented about that other alleged victim of Satanic abuse:

"Who would believe her story? Yet this is not the half of it. Some girls are forced to eat parts of their own babies."

For some time I had been endeavouring to obtain an interview with the Chief Constable of the Greater Manchester Police, Sir James Anderton. As a prominent Christian, and a police officer having to deal with allegations of human sacrifice and abuse, I felt his comments would be very valid. He replied, politely declining my offer. However, I did eventually receive answers to my queries on the 'Sarah' case, via his Superintendent Staff Officer, in a letter dated 24 January 1991. I have set out the questions and answers below. PH are my initials, and SSO refers to 'Superintendent Staff Officer'.

PH.   Can you tell me what your policy is regarding individuals who make these extreme allegations?

SSO. When an individual makes an allegation of crime it is the policy of the Greater Manchester Police to investigate the same. Any subsequent prosecution will be contingent on the circumstances and supportive evidence.

PH.   Dr Harris claims that a police surgeon has examined Sarah and has confirmed her story of suffering 'multiple rape'. Is this true?

SSO. No.

PH.   Is anyone being charged with her abduction and abuse?

SSO. No.

PH.   Sarah claims she saw the ritual murder of a temple member who had 'transgressed', and also heard the cries of babies being sacrificed. Has anyone been interviewed on this matter, have there been any arrests, and will anyone be charged?

SSO. No.

PH.   Have the Greater Manchester Police discovered any evidence that such groups are operating in the area?

SSO. No.

Is child sacrifice a fact or a fiction? Only time will tell. But time has a habit of coming in cycles. Doreen Valiente remembers similar allegations made in December 1958, by an occult investigator called Leslie Roberts.

It was during a lecture at the Adelphi Hotel in Brighton that Roberts claimed that 'black magic groups' in Rottingdean and Eastbourne were sacrificing babies. The following day, the *Brighton Evening Argus* carried the headline: POLICE PROBE "BLACK MAGIC MURDER". A statement from Mr Albert Rowsell, Brighton's Chief Constable, reads:

A few weeks ago my officers were making enquiries into another matter when they met Mr Roberts, who in the course of general conversation talked to them about black magic. In the course of the conversation Mr Roberts said he had received information that a baby had been sacrificed in a black magic ceremony at Rottingdean some time ago.

The officers concerned made some enquiries and found no corroboration of this story and it was, quite frankly, dismissed as being fantastic. But now that Mr Roberts has made a further public statement of this a full investigation will be made by the police. The matter will be treated seriously.

This caused a furore amongst the press. They besieged the police station and Roberts' flat. Eventually the Chief Constable came out with a final statement:

"The matter has been investigated to a point which enables me to say with confidence that there is no substance whatever in this matter."

Doreen Valiente agreed with the police position at the time, that it was all nonsense. She was convinced that Roberts had just got carried away with his investigations. Because of the current allegations, she says, "Today I am not so sure." This change of attitude came about through an interview with Roberts by Philip Paul, a reporter for *Psychic News*.

The most significant thing Leslie said to Philip Paul, though I did not realise it at the time, was that the baby who was the alleged victim of the black magic sacrifice was in fact a three-month foetus. He confirmed this to me afterwards, saying that the child had been aborted and that this pitiful scrap of humanity had then been used as an offering to Satan in the Black Mass.

It seems possible to me now that, considering the theory of magical ritual, a child which had been aborted might even be preferred to one which had been born in the natural way. The 'virgin parchment' so prized by sorcerers for the inscription of magical talismans is made from the skins of dead-born lambs. It is virgin because the creature has never lived in the normal sense, but it has been alive. How much more would a human baby which had never lived in the ordinary way have been regarded as 'virgin' and hence highly potent for magical purposes?

Valiente acknowledges that we may never know the truth of these matters. However, there is a historical precedent for modern allegations of aborted foetal sacrifice.

In 1678, when Nicolas de la Reynie, Louis XIV's Lieutenant-General of Police, arrested a large number of people in connection with a plague of poisoning in Versailles, he also uncovered a nest of sorcerers, priests and fortune-tellers - including the King's mistress - who were engaged in black magic ceremonies.

The sixty seven year-old priest, Guignard, was described in this way by La Reynie:

> A libertine who has travelled a great deal...and is at present attached to the Church of Saint Marcel. For twenty years he has engaged continually in the practice of poison, sacrilege and every evil business. He has cut the throats and sacrificed uncounted numbers of children on his infernal altar. He has a mistress...by whom he has had several children, one or two of whom he has sacrificed...It is no ordinary man who thinks it is natural to sacrifice infants by slitting their throats and to say Mass upon the bodies of naked women.

The black mass - a reversal of the Christian mass - is celebrated on the naked body of a woman. Central to this scandal was Madame de Montespan, who bought herself into the affections of the King through taking part in Guignard's Satanic masses - and very successfully too. She usurped his other mistresses and mothered several of his children. At the peak of her success, she was viewed by many to be as powerful as the Queen.

It was Catherine Monvoison, society sorceress, abortionist and poisoner, who introduced her to the renegade priest when various love potions had failed to win her the heart and bed of King Louis.

Monvoison was in a very good position to provide the priest with both clients and victims. As an abortionist she had a steady flow of pregnant women who wanted to get rid of their unborn children, quietly and permanently.

During these bloody rituals, Madame de Montespan would lie on her back, naked, at right angles across the altar, knees drawn up, a chalice placed between her open thighs. Guignard would stand before her, and at the height of the ceremony, slit the throat of the aborted child, allowing its blood to collect in the chalice.

Nicolas de la Reynie arrested two hundred and sixteen men and women. Of these, one hundred and ten were exiled, imprisoned or hanged. Before the scandal could taint the King, Louis stopped the investigation and his mistress retained her freedom and her life. The cover-up was not complete, however. La Reynie kept copies of all his notes and letters which were subsequently made public.

For all the talk of human sacrifice today, the evidence is conspicuous by its absence. Let us keep an open mind, but hope all the emotive rhetoric is just that; a disturbing but meaningless noise.

Chapter Ten

Witchfinders General
REACHOUT (And I'll Be There)

I see Heaven's glories shine,
And faith shines equal, arming me from fear.'
Emily Bronte

It was the morning after the burning of the night before that I set out to meet Maureen Davies, Director of Reachout Trust. A thick pall of smog suffocated the air and dulled the vision from Manchester as far west as the River Mersey. Luckily the victims who burned atop these bonfires were filled with straw and newspaper rather than the crushed and broken spirits of men, women and children of that other age. By the time I reached the outskirts of Chester the mist was dispersing, and I was shielding my eyes beneath the sunny autumnal skies of northern Wales.

Reachout is a Christian organisation concerned with victims of cult and occult groups, prepared where necessary to 'take action'. They exercise a programme of education to teach and encourage others to search out ritual perversion and take up the cudgel on behalf of Christian morality. The Trust was formalised in 1983. Maureen Davies joined two years later and eventually became a director. Currently she orchestrates the occult side of the work, on a national level. Reachout, she told me, was born out of a need that was not being met.

"Victims need a refuge where they can think for themselves. They're so brainwashed they don't know how to think. They've forfeited the right to think. They have people dictating to them what to do, what to wear, where to go. Parents ring up, friends, and tell me someone wants to 'come out' but they don't know how. Children become disturbed with ouija boards, spiritualism, traumas from Dungeons and Dragons. In America they've got forty five cases of these games linked with murder..."

Maureen Davies is fresh-faced, over-worked and serious. The three telephones in her office rarely stop ringing and consequently, she tells me, she has no patience with 'time wasters'. When she finds time to laugh, the sound has a wicked quality to it. Her crusade has taken her into television studios and onto the front pages of national newspapers, and across the Great Pond to the United States. The daughter of an Anglican vicar, she trained as a nurse, but then gained first-hand knowledge of unchristian activities:

"I became deeply involved in advanced spiritualism, so I know the very real effects these things can have on the mind."

It was after she and her husband returned to the Christian fold that they joined Reachout.

"We organised a public meeting to share with others the psychological, spiritual and physical dangers of the occult. It was very well attended, there were over four hundred people. We had medical people talking, and a person previously involved in black magic who told the audience about her experience with child sacrifice."

The gathering captured the imagination of the media, and rocketed this parochial organisation onto a par with the Childwatch charity. But Reachout does not have access to the kind of funds available to its sister group. At one stage the Freemasons offered cash, but Maureen Davies had to turn it down for political reasons:

"But I was tempted," she added.

Is she happy with the way the media are handling the witchcraft issue?

"Eighty to ninety per cent of the media are taking a more responsible role towards these very real dangers. I realise I'm speaking as a Christian, but you don't have to be one to share what is happening. The occult is like taking drugs. You can't be involved without physical, emotional and spiritual effects taking place. The media are beginning to see the truth of this, that lives are affected, people ending up in mental hospitals, committing suicide, murder. I am encouraged by the way the media are handling it. Maybe some of it is over-sensationalised; there needs to be more of a balance, but this will come."

Most of the Wiccans I have interviewed were quick to distance themselves from Satanism, claiming it has nothing to do with their pagan beliefs. Do you think they are right ?

"It all comes under the umbrella of the occult. But, yes, I think there is a difference between witchcraft and Satanism. To be a Satanist you have to have a belief system of Christianity. Witches say that Satan is a figment of the Christian imagination, but it is a belief of the Satanists. They pray to Satan as the *Lord*. White witches will not entertain Satan. But when it comes to black witches, with some of the gods they worship, then Satan must be part of that, albeit under another name. There are hundreds of these gods. For instance, 'Molech' is not the name of Satan but he is the god who demands the sacrifice of children."

This may not be entirely accurate. 2 Kings 23.10, says: 'And he defiled Topheth, which is in the valley of the sons of Hinnom, that no-one might burn his son or his daughter as an offering to Molech.' Although on the surface this seems to support Mrs Davies' statement, modern theologians believe an error of translation transformed 'Molech' into a deity, when in fact it was merely a technical term for child sacrifice conducted by the Israelites, probably to Yahweh.

'Molech' aside, do any of these gods exist - do demons exist as objective entities? It is a recurring question that I cannot resist asking yet again...

"They are very real. When you've got a child or an adult being sexually molested by an incubus, then you know it's not imagination. The number of men who are heavily into pornography, who also admit they are molested during the night is high. Well, what is it? They know they're not in bed with a woman! It is not a human being, what is it? It has got to be a demonic power."

But there is a body of opinion who will say it is 'psychological', fulfilling a need.

"What would you say to someone who doesn't want to have sex with one of these things? Is that a psychological need? They don't have a choice...We've come across many of these cases, and for psychologists to say there is a need, I find very insulting."

Do you think that innocent people become involved in black witchcraft unwittingly, then later turn to child abuse, or is it a case of psychopaths and paedophiles joining such groups to further their perversions?

"The people we've counselled have been made to take part. They are actually very distressed because they've been ordered to do it."

You mentioned earlier a lady who claimed she had actually witnessed child sacrifice. Is this Audrey Harper ?

"Yes."

During *The Time, The Place*, Audrey Harper said the police were not interested in her child sacrifice stories.

"She has been interviewed by the police. It's all above board."

Are there going to be some arrests ? She can obviously name names.

"No she can't! In these circles they all adopt other names. You don't know who's who."

Surely over a period of time she would have got to know the other coven members?

"No, she didn't. The politics of the covens mean they are not an open community."

On that same programme, a man, introduced as a Satanist, had a crime he committed some years previously exposed by journalist John Merry. What can you tell me about that? Someone has told me it was a set-up. Or was it spontaneous?

Mrs Davies started smiling then burst into laughter.

"I can't comment on that. I think John Merry just knew something which other people didn't."

And he wanted to make it known?

More laughter.

"Before the programme began a few of us had a meeting."

Do you think it was a good thing he was exposed?

"I think it was good to bring to the surface something which was known. He was the only one paid to appear on the programme."

John Merry is another witchfinder. Grey-haired, and stockily built, he has a dominating manner to go with his stature. He is an investigative journalist with a Newcastle newspaper called *The Sunday Sun*, and, over the last eight years, has been responsible for many exposés of occultists allegedly practising black witchcraft. During *The Time, The Place*, he dominated the discussion to such an extent that at one point Mike Scott, the presenter, had to reassert control.

Merry is a man with a bee in his bonnet, and while he thinks that occult powers are illusory, he has no illusions about the reality of ritual abuse, without going to the outer edges of human sacrifice and murder allegation. He believes that the covens and temples of black witches and Satanists are a convenient cover for illegal practices and 'sexual perversion'. This is what he said on *The Time, The Place*:

"Quite frankly you're not looking at Satanism, and you're not looking at spells, but outrageous perverts! You are looking at people who are using other people's bodies to satisfy their sexual lust. You're talking about outrageous perverts who are prepared to interfere with children for the satisfaction of their sexual lust."

When pushed about ritual murder, he replied:

"I must state categorically that I have never come across any case of human sacrifice. I have absolutely no evidence for that whatsoever."

However, people like John Merry, Maureen Davies and Dianne Core of Childwatch are convinced there is a serious problem, and it is only a matter of time before it is proven.

Dianne Core operates in the North East, and is convinced that all these assertions are true. In a filmed interview for ITN, Ms Core said:

"We are getting evidence of this type of Satanic activity with children from all over the British Isles. As we go deeper and do more research it's a bit like Pandora's box - the more we open the lid the more comes out."

She claimed that a national scandal was only being averted through a lack of direct evidence. In a feature published in the October 1988 issue of *SHE* magazine Ms Core told the writer, Bill Williamson, of three children "snatched from a coven". There, they were allegedly forced to eat excrement and drink urine, before being tied onto an inverted cross for use in perverted sex sessions. Why, then was no 'direct evidence' obtained in this case? When it comes to 'normal' child abuse cases, the police seem very good at collating evidence and carrying out prosecutions.

But what of the Church, I asked Maureen Davies?

"I am the first to acknowledge that the Church has got its own problems. Statements have been made that there's more molestation in the Church than with Satanists. I admit that. I'm not looking for excuses, and I'm certainly not here to hide things. But ordinary sex abuse, even though it is horrendous, is fairly straight-forward compared to the abuse which goes on in Satanist groups."

Do you think the re-introduction of legislation to outlaw witchcraft would help ?

"No. The legislation we had up to 1951 didn't stop it - but we do need a change in the law to recognise Satanic crime. Currently this is not recognised in our legal system. Being involved in the occult can damage your health.

"You cannot experience mind-bending manipulative powers and remain unaffected. You can't try LSD and say your mind's the same afterwards. Whatever type of person becomes involved in the occult, after six months they will have undergone a personality change. The spirit behind all of this is to control, dominate. Once in a coven, you're the one who dominates, or you're the one who is dominated. Some men enjoy being dominated and controlled."

Do you think a lot of people become embroiled in it through family links?

"Not as many compared with those who independently choose to join. The evil powers from Satan come to kill, maim and turn whatever is pure impure. It is totally destructive. The biggest gift you can give Satan is to give yourself in sacrifice. And these people consider it is an honour. This has got to be a perverted belief system, but that is how brainwashed they are."

These stories in the tabloid press of human sacrifice intrigue me greatly, but at the end of the day all we have is a story, and one person's word for it. A lot of people must read these stories and wonder how much of it is made up because there are no facts.

"But if the lid was taken off it now we couldn't handle it. The Church isn't ready, neither are the police. So you see, I'm not really worried. It needs to leak out so that you are convincing the people who need to be convinced."

Do you think the problem is getting worse, or is it being contained?

"The problem is getting worse because there are more recruitment problems now. But the problem has always been there. Who would believe some of the things which go on? Some victims are carted off to the mental asylum - it is so bizarre!"

And that is the problem the police have got. It *is* so bizarre. They've got to have proof - unequivocal proof. There have got to be facts, and there do not seem to be enough facts.

"We know of thirty five cases which are being investigated. I'm not discouraged by lack of facts. There can't be this much information coming out without a prosecution somewhere sticking. It has to happen."

But the Big Break hasn't happened, has it ?

"The big break we are absolutely looking for - no. Not as the press would like it. There was a conference at Reading University where child abuse was on the agenda, so people are listening."

The conference, held at the university, though not organised by it, took place in September 1989. It was attended by many social workers and child health specialists. They were told of children being lured into covens and forced to take part in perverted sex and drink the blood of sacrifice victims. Many came away convinced.

Isn't there a big danger that the whole thing will blow up into a real witch hunt ?

"I don't think anyone is getting involved in a 'witch hunt'. The only thing we did was carry out some research to find out what was available and where. I don't see a witch hunt. We're too busy dealing with the victims.

"Our biggest problem is convincing other Christians there is a problem. They sit back in their holy haloes, very comfortable, don't rock the boat please, don't bring the dirt and muck in our church. They are certainly no threat to Satan !"

She laughs again, that same laugh.

"The Church has got to start being the Church it is supposed to be. The time for playing at Christianity has finished."

Before I left, Mrs Davies handed me a circular she had written entitled SATANIC RITUAL ABUSE. Under the subheading; SYMPTOMS THAT CHILDREN SHOW AS A RESULT OF RITUAL ABUSE, the following points are included:

They may have an obsession about urine and faeces and if young have difficulty being toilet trained. This is because they think it may be collected, and later they will have to eat it or it will be plastered over their body.

A morbid curiosity with death, wondering if everyone eats dead people or cuts them up. These children do not ask normal questions about death that a child would.

The children play aggressively and have pleasures in hurting people. They destroy toys and may act out what they have seen in the rituals.

Harming animals or wanting to kill them.

Reciting nursery rhymes with indecent overtones.

Suffering from severe nightmares, bed wetting.

They may have a fear of snakes, beetles and insects especially as these are associated in their minds with pain and perversion.

What are we to make of this catalogue of horror? What child at some stage does not have a fascination with bodily functions? How many parents can say they had no difficulty in toilet training their children? How many children, especially at nursery, do not occasionally play aggressively or break a toy? How many parents of five year-olds have not heard their son or daughter recite 'indecent' verses picked up in the playground? Which child does not have nightmares and bed wetting, or fears snakes?

Another horror exists counter to the beliefs of today's witchfinders. That horror is that their allegations of bestial ritual abuse will prove ultimately unfounded. If that turns out to be the case, what does it say about them?

Chapter Eleven

BURNING

You shall not practice augury or witchcraft. Do not turn to mediums or wizards; do not seek them out, to be defiled by them: I am the LORD your God. A man or a woman who is a medium or a wizard shall be put to death; they shall be stoned with stones, their blood shall be upon them. Leviticus 19-20

It is dark, and quiet, in a street in Leeds, early in the morning of 13 August 1989. Close to the park there is a shop; The Sorcerer's Apprentice. It is squat and brooding in the darkness. Someone approaches the door and smashes through the plate glass, the destructive sound rippling through the terraced streets, pricking those in slumber. What ? Where? Wonder drowsy minds, before sinking into the abyss of sleep once more.

Silence again, then the snap! snap! of bolt cutters working on the security grill behind the shattered door. Then they are in.

Violence erupts. In a frenzy, shelves containing books by Aleister Crowley are ripped from the wall. Opposite, more shelves are attacked, hacked and splintered into ruin. Crowley's tomes, together with books on witchcraft, are piled in the middle of the shop floor. No other books are touched. A match flares to life. The burning begins...

The witchcraft controversy was ripe for investigation. So many claims and counter-claims had been made that it needed a thorough going over by responsible investigative journalists who would present the facts. It needed it, but it did not get it. Instead, the controversy was further clouded by Roger Cook with *The Devil's Work*, which was eventually broadcast on 17 July 1989.

Roger Cook has earned a reputation in Britain for pursuing the rich and the powerful suspected of ripping off the public with phoney insurance policies, non-existent holiday homes and substandard building work. Nothing is more satisfying than seeing a bully receive his just deserts, even if in the process, Cook himself might suffer the occasional fractured jaw. But his excursion into the witchcraft conflict was a sad mistake. Scheduled originally for showing on 22 May, it was postponed for cuts and a later viewing slot, although some cynics said it was because Cook was having a problem finding enough material. Indeed, according to the *Daily Star* of 3 May, Roger Cook imported into Britain American Satanist leader, Michael Aquino and his wife, Lillith, for filming, on an all expenses paid trip. This prompted Dianne Core, who provided material for the programme, to exclaim to the *Star*:

"It is horrendous that Roger Cook brought him into this country when we are fighting to keep him out!"

The show itself convinced no-one. And that is a shame. It was a lost opportunity. Cook, grossly overweight, mumbled and bumbled his way through the footage looking more and more like Benny Hill. Black witchcraft took second place to black comedy in the shape of the afore-mentioned Aquinos. Dressed to kill in make-up and costumes more at home on the set of *The Munsters*, the odd couple inaugurated David Austin, a chef and former National Front member, into The Temple of Set. Cook accused them of child abuse, and they denied it. There was never any proof produced one way or another. Viewers were left hanging.

The Reverend Logan was filmed in his church with some young people allegedly damaged by witchcraft, Chris Bray was chased around the streets of Leeds in Hallowe'en mask, and the

familiar allegations of child sacrifice were made. The following
day the critics lost no time in drawing blood;

> Roger Cook has definitely gone off the boil. His *Cook Report
> Special* had more holes in it than Keith Floyd's colander.
> "Satanism is going through an explosion" said a Lancashire vicar
> who sounded more like a satellite dish salesman. His 30-minute
> television shows are now sensational, trivial and lacking re-
> search. *Yorkshire Evening Post*

> The techniques of down-market tabloid newspapers do not
> translate easily to the television screen. But when they are
> successfully copied, the consequences of the transfer make one
> see why few people want free-for-all TV. Mr Cook's producers
> have been persuaded, with little hard evidence beyond a collec-
> tion of newspaper stories, that there had been an 'explosion' of
> belief in Satanism. A distressing child abuse case in Nottingham,
> was cited with a social worker stating that it involved Satanism.
> This assertion was promptly denied by the police. *Daily Mail*

> Here is Ozzy Osbourne hastily back-pedalling on the mythology
> after a clip of his song celebrating our old Satanist friend Aleister
> Crowley: "I am not a devil worshipper, I have never been
> involved in black magic - it takes me all my time to conjure
> myself out of bed, let alone conjure up the devil." *The Guardian*

The programme even managed to upset homosexuals as
illustrated by this letter published in the *TV Times* of 2 September:

> "I was distressed by a remark made by an ex-Satanist who
> lectured people about the dangers of becoming involved in such
> sects. She said these groups attracted 'homosexuals, lesbians
> and paedophiles'. I am deeply upset by this remark because it
> implies that all gays and lesbians are evil and should be feared..."

Other reviewers remarked that the style of presentation of the
subject would only attract new adherents. Of those who provided
background material for the programme, others, apart from

Dianne Core, were less than satisfied with the outcome. This is what the Reverend Logan told me:

"In one sense it was disappointing. It didn't reveal enough, and the comical aspects detracted from its seriousness."

Maureen Davies had mixed feelings:

"There are two sides to *The Cook Report*. Those who think not enough was exposed, and those who had never heard of ritual abuse and thought it was too heavy. After that programme we had over four hundred phone calls, mainly from Satanists wanting to come out. Even though there were ten people manning the phones that night, it was not enough for us to listen to them; they wanted some practical advice."

It was not surprising that the programme failed. Cook and his team were out of their depth. The back-bone of any investigative documentary is good solid research backed up with facts. My experience of television researchers is that they do very little original work, but rely instead on the unpaid help of 'contacts'. Cook and researcher Tim Tate obviously had no understanding at all of the utter complexity of the occult subject. So they gathered together a string of scary stories, then climbed on the treadmill of Dennis Wheatley stereotypes, and produced thirty minutes of tabloid journalism. That is a shame, for those of us who were sitting back waiting for the facts on a supposed international scandal.

Someone else was not pleased with *The Devil's Work* either: occultist and owner of The Sorcerer's Apprentice and Astonishing Books, Mr Christopher Bray.

Bray was told by Dianne Core as long ago as April 1988, that *The Cook Report* were planning a programme on ritual child abuse. In December, through his solicitors, he wrote to Central Television expressing his concern. On 31 January, Tim Tate replied, requesting a filmed interview for inclusion in the programme. Part of this letter read:

"Please be assured it is not our intention to subject you (or the occult in general) to what your solicitors term 'misinformed vilification'."

In a letter dated 10 February 1989, on Bray's instructions, his solicitors wrote that because previous interviews had been misrepresented, their client would not be interviewed on camera, and neither would he give permission for his premises to be filmed:

> Nonetheless our client does wish *The Cook Report* to be able to obtain all the facts in order to present the truth to the public so that those engaged in criminal conduct may be brought to justice whether or not they use occultism as a guide for their practices. Our client is therefore prepared to supply information to *The Cook Report* without charge providing such information is used for the purposes of research for the programme only and not used either in part or in whole as a part of the programme itself.

Apparently, Tim Tate did not take up the offer, and instead, accompanied Cook and a large camera crew to Bray's shop on 2 May. Their aim was to confront him about passages in certain books and magazines he sold which seemed to promote human sacrifice as part of witchcraft ritual. Bray claims the passages were quoted out of context. He also claims that he does not sell to people under eighteen, although, as most of his business is done through mail order, I cannot see how he can be so certain.

On the day in question, Bray describes in a public information sheet what happened;

> *The Cook Report* DOORSTEPPED the Sorcerer's Apprentice in the usual abominable fashion which really should be outlawed. Laying siege to our premises, first with concealed cameras and then with three camera crews, one in front, one at the side and one at the rear of the building. Altogether there were over a dozen TV people present including Cook's minders.

Mr Bray called the police, but eventually decided to close the premises for the day. He and his staff disguised in fancy dress, drove away after a final attempt at interview by the persistent Roger Cook.

Bray claims he is innocent, and that he was deliberately victimised by *The Cook Report* on behalf of Christian fundamentalists because of his influential position in providing books and witchcraft paraphernalia to occultists all over Europe. He believes there was a conspiracy between the programme-makers and fundamentalists to blacken the name of occultism with 'phantom allegations' dressed up as fact. I wrote to Central Television for their side of the story, and received a reply from Jonathan Holder, their legal adviser. He thanked me for my letter, but said it was inappropriate for Roger Cook to reply while Mr Bray's complaint was being considered by the Broadcasting Complaints Commission.

For the previous eighteen months, Bray had been contacting newspapers, the Home Office and the police in an effort to counteract what he sees as a "combined conspiracy by the Xtians" with their "phantom allegations on child abuse" to start up a "Xtian Holy War". He had warned about a threat to public order because of the allegations. Sure enough, four weeks after *The Devil's Work*, almost to the day, Bray's shop was mysteriously gutted by fire.

Bray of course has laid the blame at the feet of Christian 'fanatics'. The Reverend Logan made this comment.

"By definition, whoever started that fire could not be a Christian. Besides, there is speculation concerning the exact source of the fire."

Was the fire an inside or an outside job?

As if pre-empting such allegations, Christopher Bray said this in a public statement:

"I confidently expect that, before long, the fundamentalists will accuse me of setting fire to my own shop for political reasons."

Several days before the burning, Maureen Davies gave a lecture in nearby Wakefield. Bray speculated that this might have incited the perpetrators of the fire, and confided his suspicions to the police. When I spoke to her, Mrs Davies was none too pleased.

"After the fire, the police came and interviewed me. Bray had put my name on his list of suspects! That was dangerous, because if anyone believed I'd had anything to do with it, the same thing could happen here."

On 6 December, Bray attended a meeting in London of the Broadcasting Complaints Commission chaired by Lady Anglesey. Also present were Roger Cook, Tim Tate and producer Mike Townson. Mr Bray seemed very pleased by the way the meeting went:

"It went well for me that despite the usual Establishment conditioning facts and questions were put which *The Cook Report* had either buried or did not consider for their programme. It showed their involvement to be entirely sensational in intent. The *CR* team were noticeably shaken and at last began to see what it was they had involved themselves in."

The adjudication took several months, and Bray's version of it appeared in a pamphlet edited by 'John Freedom' called *Bad News*. The entire February 1990 edition was given over to the controversy, headlined: 'COOK REPORT EXPOSED - BCC Censures CTV - Devil's Work biased and unfair.' The report began:

The government inaugurated Broadcasting Complaints Commission has at long last bared its teeth in a ferocious attack upon both Central Television and the IBA in the adjudication of a complaint against Roger Cook's controversial *The Devil's Work* screened during July 1989.

Much of the rest of the account in *Bad News* was ambiguous, in the sense that a casual reader might assume that opinions expressed by the editor and Mr Bray were also the opinions of the BCC. I obtained the full adjudication from the Broadcasting

Complaints Commission some weeks later, and this is what it actually says:

> The Commission are satisfied that *The Devil's Work* was concerned with an issue of public interest and that the programme was based on evidence of ritualistic crime committed in the name of Satanism. They did not interpret the programme as implying that every Satanist was a child abuser or involved in ritualistic crime. The programme did not purport to be an extensive investigation into Satanism. The Commission do not consider that it is for them to determine whether Satanism either attracts or encourages people who have a propensity to commit such acts despite references in the programme to this danger. Apart from Roger Cook's admitted reference to witchcraft when questioning Mr Bray, the programme did not appear to confuse other aspects of the occult with Satanism. They do not consider that the programme associated the occult in general with child sexual abuse.
>
> The Commission consider it evident that Mr Bray's shop and the publications sold there are a major source of material by and for Satanists as well as other branches of the occult. Some of the articles he had published were, as the programme suggested, dubious in their content and some of his editorial comments were ambiguous. While the Commission accept that a publisher of the kind of diverse material dealt with in the programme may not be responsible or answerable for the ideas behind it, they nevertheless consider that he cannot be immune from criticism and can reasonably be asked for comment. The Commission consider that the programme makers were justified on the grounds of public interest in seeking to obtain information from Mr Bray and that there was no unwarranted infringement of his privacy. The Commission do find that the programme was unfair to him in as much as Roger Cook's questions to him could have been taken by the viewer to associate Mr Bray personally with child sexual abuse. However, the Commission do not find that the programme was unfair to occultism in general.

Mr Bray has since set up a fighting fund to finance his 'holy war'. He is now concerned with organising a private meeting between Geoffrey Dickens and Home Office Minister, John Patten. The purpose of the meeting was a proposed amendment to the Criminal Justice Bill to make it illegal for people under eighteen to 'join, participate in or be present at any secret occult ceremonies or groups'. Occultists claim this would be in breach of Article 18 of the United Nations Universal Declaration of Human Rights. Chris Bray warned journalist, Rosie Waterhouse:

"If the Government, through political expediency or ignorance, allows this amendment, they should be in no doubt that we will take a trial case to the European Court of Human Rights."

Chapter Twelve

SPECTRAL EVIDENCE

As I was walking down the stair
I met a man who was not there
He was not there again today
I wish that man would go away.

In 1987, the witchcraft allegations took a quantum leap when social workers acted where police could not, or would not tread. As we have seen, essentially, the police need evidence of a crime in order to act. Social workers, with the welfare of children constantly in mind, need only to have just reason of belief. Children are taken from natural parents and held in the care of foster parents while police search for evidence to bring about a prosecution. Often social workers are in a no-win situation: If they do not act quickly and a child suffers or even dies they are condemned; if they take a child away, and later, sometimes months later, the allegations of abuse are proven unfounded, they are criticised for being over-zealous. All in all it is a thankless and stressful job. They rummage around in a pit of misery, wading through a mire of base human thoughts and actions, constantly facing the possibility of personal physical violence.

If the physical and sexual abuse of children were not horrific enough, an added dimension has dragged their investigations down into new realms of depravity. Groups of social workers in the midlands and north of England were persuaded that an organised network of adults were using children in ritual acts as part of an anti-Christian belief system. The officially unrecognised terms, 'Satanic abuse' and 'ritual abuse' began to appear in newspaper reports based on interviews with these workers.

In Liverpool and Alfreton, Derbyshire, children, allegedly abused and showing 'a fear of the Devil', were put into care. Police and social workers swooped on an estate in Manchester and took away thirteen children. This case, heard at Manchester High Court, ended after eleven weeks on 18 December 1990.

Although Mr Justice Hollings decided all thirteen must remain wards of court, he ruled that eight of them could live with their parents, albeit under intensive professional supervision, but five others had to stay in council care. Manchester's Director of Social Services, Michael Bishop, formerly director of social services in Cleveland at the height of the child abuse furore, claimed the judges decision was a victory for his department. But Mr Hollings was critical of the actions of the social workers. There were some very elementary and unprofessional mistakes made.

He criticised them for becoming immersed in a belief system of real Satanic ritual abuse, for telling children what other children had said at interview, and said that no research had been carried out to ensure the children were not creating fantasies from information gleaned from books, magazines and videos. Of the five children remaining in care, he commented:

"There was probable abuse of a sadistic nature in bogus ritual circumstances, probably by more than one adult."

But these cases were really a sideline to two others which captured national headlines and caused a storm of debate: Nottingham and Rochdale.

Lynchpin of the occult/child abuse interface was an upcoming trial involving a large number of adults in Nottingham. According to various interested parties, including Geoffrey Dickens, this would present unambiguous proof that practising occultists were involved in abuse.

In 1989, nine adults, all but one from the same extended family, were imprisoned for up to ten years on fifty three charges of incest. It had taken three years to bring the case to court. The family lived on the Broxtowe council estate on the edge of Nottingham. At one stage twenty five children were in care. Many of them had been raped while their young relatives were made to watch. It was horrible, it was punished, but at that stage that is all it was - 'ordinary' child abuse.

About a year after the initial arrests, one of the children began telling his foster mother stories about snakes and monsters. This was reported back to Nottingham Social Services Department. Similar stories began to emerge from some of the other Broxtowe children. They told of people wearing witch's costumes, jumping on a doll, drinking blood in a church and animal sacrifice.

The Social Services Department set up 'Team 4' to deal with it. It was headed by Judith Dawson, Principal Professional Officer (Child Protection). She came into contact with Christian fundamentalists and was convinced that Team 4 was dealing with Satanic abuse. As with so many things extreme, the term had originated in America. Detective Gerry Simandi of the Chicago Police Department, defined it at the Reading University conference in September 1989:

"Repeated physical, emotional, mental and spiritual assaults on children, combined with a systematised use of symbols and ceremonies and the use of evil, designed and orchestrated to attain harmful effects - to turn the victims against themselves, society and God."

At that same conference, according to Heather Rutt, secretary of St Albans Community Health Council, Judith Dawson and Nottingham colleague, Christine Johnson, gave horrific details of the children's allegations.

According to a lengthy article in *The Mail on Sunday*, dated 21 October 1990, not all the social workers in Nottingham were in accord with the conclusions of those in Team 4. One who disagreed alleges she was subsequently 'isolated'. She told *Mail* reporters:

"There was a buzz of excitement around. There was no doubt some people realised that if they could prove ritual abuse existed in Britain, they could publish, give lectures, and generally become eminent in their field."

It was decided that other 'evidence' of Satanic abuse should be obtained and collated from the other Broxtowe children. Team 4 decided that instead of obtaining the information via the usual channel of formal interviews, it should be left up to the foster mothers. To prepare them for this task, the mothers attended a briefing by Chicago evangelist, and 'psychologist', Pam Klein, a colleague of Gerry Simandi. Ms Klein is a controversial figure in America, where a judge has ruled that she is "not a legitimate therapist", as defined by Illinois law. However, she does hold a bachelor's degree in sociology and psychology and a master's degree in counselling education. Both here and in America she has been actively involved in cases of alleged Satanic abuse.

Thus prepared, the women went about soliciting information from their young charges. Some of the children drew pictures depicting fairy tale witches. Of one child, her foster mother commented:

"She used to say little bits, then those bits would get longer."

John Newsom, Professor of Child Development at Nottingham University, commented on the methodology of Team 4:

"I became concerned at the degree to which words were being put into children's mouths - strong insistence and assertion being used and the alternation of a sympathetic and a forceful attitude. If they, the foster parents, were strong evangelical Christians, they might take a different view to atheistic, less convinced believers in Hell and the Devil."

Nevertheless, Team 4 pressed Nottingham police to re-open the case. They presented them with a list of other adults not originally arrested, who Team 4 claimed had committed Satanic abuse in cemeteries, particularly the Rock Cemetery on Mansfield Road. Christine Johnson, a social worker connected with Team 4, had this to say:

"We told the police this described ceremonies in which the children were abused. They immediately said; there is no witchcraft in Nottingham. You'll lose the case for us. Just concentrate on the sexual abuse, we don't want to know about anything else."

According to Ms Johnson, when this additional information was placed before appeal Judge Mrs Justice Booth, she supported Team 4 in their conclusions. She described what had happened to the children as 'Satanic'. However, after investigation, the police decided not to take action. Sergeant Beeton, the officer who brought the original case to court, commented:

"Although connection with the occult was a feature of the case, there was absolutely no evidence to support the allegation."

Team 4 then asked the Department of Health for an external inquiry. Instead Team 4 itself was investigated! The inquiry team consisted of three senior social workers and three high-ranking police officers, plus outside advisers such as Professor Newsom. Eventually a report was produced, which included a dozen alternative explanations to the one held by Team 4 that children were being abused as part of rituals practised by a network of Satanists.

Judith Dawson would not talk to me or provide material for this book, but she was happy to take part in a documentary for Channel 4. As part of the *Dispatches* series, *Listen To The Children* was broadcast on 3 October 1990. Produced and fronted by journalist, Beatrix Campbell, it consisted of interviews with Team 4, several 'experts' and reconstructions using child actors. The reconstructions were in respect of two locations where some of the children claimed they had been abused during Satanic rituals; Rock Cemetery and Wollaton Hall.

Beatrix Campbell and a camera crew went into some tunnels beneath the cemetery, tunnels which the police claimed they had already searched without finding anything. The eerie atmosphere was hyped up by Ms Campbell's use of a domestic torch, rather than the powerful lights usually used by film crews. In between gasps and utterances of "Oh my goodness..." we were treated to pictures of partly used candles in sooty niches and symbols scratched onto the walls.

At Wollaton Hall, a child described how she and other children had been abused in basement rooms. Team 4 were certain she could not have described the rooms without having been there. In the programme, the police were accused of suppressing or ignoring evidence of Satanic abuse. Towards the end of the programme, Ms Campbell resorted to her electric torch once more, and the affair threatened to dissolve into farce.

In what seemed to be a carefully staged performance, she crept into the cemetery lodge which had been conveniently left unlocked. In a voice barely above a whisper, she informed us:

"We've been given information that if we were to come here we might be able to get in easily, and we might find things of interest. So we've come to explore a property. That, like the cemetery tunnels, should have been fully investigated by the police."

Lying around the room she 'found' a sex contact magazine, a video camera manual, a book on flagellation and a vibrator which looked so new it could still have had the price tag on it. The finds were punctuated by shocked utterances and indrawn breaths. On picking up a booklet on fostering and adoption Ms Campbell could not contain herself.

"Oh my goodness me! Why are they interested in fostering children?"

The programme reached a predictable level of extremism when an elderly woman, related to those imprisoned, told the reporter that not only did child abuse take place, but also child sacrifice. She claimed that after a sacrifice, an existing grave was partly dug up, and the remains placed in it. She was unable to pinpoint which graves contained the murdered children.

Despite the theatrics, *Listen To The Children* generated major newspaper articles the following day. *The Independent* published the reaction of Dan Crompton, the Chief Constable of Nottinghamshire. He reasserted that the police had searched both the tunnels and Wollaton Hall when the allegations were first brought to their attention by Team 4.

"Apart from animal bones in a cellar under Wollaton Hall, no material of significance was found."

Apparently, even these had a prosaic explanation. They were from a natural history museum. In reference to the earlier investigation of Team 4, he added that they had not provided any additional evidence that Satanism had been practised by adults, leading to the abuse of children.

In response, Team 4 claimed that Satanic abuse was taking place in five sites around Nottingham, and that they had a list of fifteen new cases linked to the earlier prosecutions. In the article, Dan Crompton raised a very important point: Research shows that abused children are likely to become abusers themselves. Extrapolating from this, he made the following very important observation:

"If, as we believe, the police are correct and these children were the object of sexual abuse, but not Satanic abuse, what will be the effect of years of 'treatment' for Satanic abuse? Are we in danger of creating a generation of Satanic/ritualistic abusers ?"

The New Statesman took up the cudgel on behalf of Team 4 and blamed 'police culture' for the lack of positive police action. Only *The Independent on Sunday*, and *The Mail on Sunday* showed a continuity of scepticism over the social workers' claims. Indeed, the latter illustrated how flawed some of the children's stories were after investigation.

Several children told Team 4 that sheep had been slaughtered at a certain address. Police forensic scientists failed to find a single speck of blood, or a strand of sheep hair in the untidy and dirty house.

Scars were noticed on the stomach of a young girl by her foster mother. The woman pressed her for an explanation. Under pressure, she said the scar had been caused by a stanley knife. She had been cut during a ritual by a female member of the family. This story was confirmed by another girl, who, according to the authors, was also at the centre of other claims. When the police investigated, they were able to demonstrate that it was untrue. The scar was the result of an exploratory operation for a congenital rupture weakness.

The Mail reported on a three year-old boy taken into care in December 1986, who they said was the catalyst of many of the later stories of Satanic rituals. He awoke one night in the throes of a nightmare, and told his foster mother that he had been reliving the horror of seeing a baby tortured. The baby's name was 'Gemma'. This mother told another foster mother who was looking after a child from the same extended family. This child knew of Gemma, but said she was an older child. Other children were asked about Gemma, and some of them knew her too. She was variously described as a baby, a young child, an eleven year-old and an adult. Gemma was black and white, lived at three different addresses, but they all agreed, that Gemma had suffered the worst atrocities in the hands of the black witches.

According to the article, the police put all their resources into finding Gemma, including the use of a Home Office computer, used in major criminal investigations. Finally they concluded that Gemma did not exist, yet *The Mail* claims that Gemma is still listed on Team 4's 'At Risk' Register.

It is all very extraordinary. Just what is the truth? David White, Director of Social Services in Nottingham, had banned the social workers in Team 4 from speaking to the media. When they agreed to be filmed for *Dispatches* they knew the risks they were taking. Jane McDermott, Acting Senior Social Worker for Team 4, knew they might lose their jobs, but she felt it was more important to protect the children. It was in that programme that her colleague, Judith Dawson, seemed perhaps to be beginning to see beyond the picture that had been fervently impressed upon them by American and British Christian fundamentalists.

"These children have been grossly sexually abused within their families, and by friends and lodgers. There were people using some kind of belief system to abuse them, some sort of Satanic group. Or were they involved in a pornographic ring using Satanic belief to further frighten the children?"

Whichever answer is correct, the phenomenon continued to sweep the country, up into the Pennines at Rochdale.

In Rochdale, the witch hunt began in March 1990, when four children from the same family were taken into care by social services after teachers reported the gory claims of a six year-old boy. The disturbed boy, who took to hiding in cupboards in the school, explained how he had been caged during rituals carried out by witches. The witches wore white cloaks and carried burning crosses while babies were put to death in local grave-yards. His ten year-old sister partly corroborated the story, but said she had witnessed the events 'in dreams'.

A search of the house by police uncovered a makeshift wooden cross in a toy cupboard. Social workers seized on the 'evidence' and applied to the High Court to make the children wards of court. Wardship was granted. The parents strongly denied they were involved in black witchcraft, and Detective Superintendent Jim Smellie head of Rochdale CID told the *Manchester Evening News*:

"We found no firm evidence to substantiate any charges being made at this stage. We did find a cross at the house but there was no evidence that it was linked to Satanism or Devil worship. It could have been entirely innocent. We would consider taking action if evidence became available."

The next step offered up predictable results, results we have already encountered in sixteenth-century Salem and Pendle, and in twentieth-century Nottingham and Manchester.

The two eldest children, when interviewed by social workers, gave a list of names of cousins and friends who were also alleged victims of occult practices. In a series of dawn raids, these children too were taken into care, their parents left vainly protesting their innocence. Eventually, twenty children had been taken away from their parents. Six were allowed home. As in Nottingham, they were all from the same council estate, although not all from the same extended family.

After five months of silence, the Social Services Department issued a three-page statement in answer to criticisms from parents and councillors. Councillor Peter Thomson in particular, was certain he knew where the childrens' stories had originated. They could be traced, he said, to twelve horror videos. These films, too horrific even for late night television viewing, are available to very young children on hire by irresponsible parents. Councillor Thomson said in his statement:

"Every allegation made of occult practices can be directly traced to scenes in these films. What the children saw was film and not their own experience. The allegations about wizards in white cloaks came from a film about the Ku Klux Klan. The children were never involved in witchcraft or Satanism. It has all been a horrible mistake.

"The children and their families are victims of guilt by association. From the time they were taken into care they were subject to constant questioning. None of the parents have been charged with any offence because I don't believe there is a scrap of medical evidence. The families are totally incapable of any of the things which are alleged. They are not followers of a Satanic cult, but they have been stripped of their children."

He also pointed out that the parents were poor and inarticulate, and thus unable to combat a system which blinded them with bureaucracy.

The official statement from the Social Services Department detailed the allegations, which now also included animal sacrifice and the administering of drugs. Social Services Director, Gordon Littlemore, had no doubts that the stories were real objective experiences, not rooted in horror video films. His beliefs were also shared by Rochdale Council's Chief Executive, John Pierce:

"Until these allegations surfaced, I had no idea things like this could be part of anybody's life. As a parent I am absolutely horrified and deeply concerned."

Critics claimed the Social Services was heading for another Cleveland-style fiasco, but Gordon Littlemore said the comparison was inappropriate, as the Cleveland cases were solely concerned with sexual abuse. However, Sue Amphlett, director of Parents Against Injustice, thought there were strong parallels with Cleveland. She also claimed that children who watched video nasties often interpreted them as a reality in which they directly played a part. What of the parents, what did they have to say? Most of them preferred to keep their heads down in case it prejudiced chances of having their children back. One couple, however, parents of three children taken into care, were prepared to talk to journalist Matt Finnegan, covering the case for the *Manchester Evening News*:

"All we know is that we sold this other couple a dog and became friends with them. They have had their children taken away and that's the only reason we can think why we have been brought into this. We have never had anything to do with witchcraft or Satanism or any other nonsense. It's ludicrous. The three of them were sobbing as they took them away. Our lives have been smashed. We don't know why and we want our children back."

Mail on Sunday journalists, Iain Walker, John Quinn and Peter Day, commented about one of the children, given the pseudonym of 'Jenny', and bemoaned the fact that an injunction was stopping them from presenting the full facts of the case to the public.

We have got to know her family very well indeed. We say, without equivocation, that they have never been involved in Satanism or similar practices. It appears that another child was asked by social workers to identify friends. She named Jenny.

Both the media and Rochdale councillors were prevented from learning full details of the case because of the legal ban. This legal 'cover-up' only reinforced fears in some quarters that a Cleveland-style mistake had been made. Bits and pieces of information leaked out into the press nevertheless. In September it was announced that parents were prevented from seeing their children even under supervision. One little girl's birthday came and went, and her parents were not even allowed to send her a card. The reason for this ban was the priming of social workers by fundamentalists. They believed that the parents, as members of a Satanic temple, would use trigger words and hand signs to silence the children.

Solicitors were appealing to the High Court to allow access. There was speculation that the entire affair was going to cost the tax-payer two million pounds in legal fees. In the midst of all this, three children in Salford were taken from their parents. There was talk from an unnamed source of professional people rubbing shoulders with occupants of a run-down estate, as part of an occult sect operating in the area. However, while some evidence of abuse was discovered, no evidence was found to support the children's allegations of occult practices.

Towards the end of September Manchester City Council effectively 'sacked' the NSPCC by withdrawing its annual £100,000 grant. The organisation was responsible for managing the child protection register and organising case conferences. The charity was accused of keeping inaccurate and out-of-date information. Case details were missing, and sometimes there was a delay in deleting names from the register. The NSPCC had taken a leading role in the investigation of the Manchester Satanic abuse case.

At the same time, the Rochdale case was switched to the High Court in London, such was its seriousness. There, Lord Justice Stephen Brown studied over seventy hours of video-taped interviews between the children and social workers, to see whether more information could be released to the media, and decide whether parents would be allowed to visit their off-spring. He was not briefed to examine the Satanic aspect of the allegations. The now retired Chief Constable of Greater Manchester, confirmed Christian, Sir James Anderton, had already said that the evidence did not justify prosecuting the parents. The judge decided to allow access, under strict supervision, to the parents of two of the children.

Then, in an about-turn that shocked Rochdale councillors, the media and the public at large, Social Services Director, Gordon Littlemore, announced that the case was not linked to Satanism! Even more astounding, he told reporters that his department had never used the terms 'Satanism' or 'Devil worship'. Yet the media had carried interviews with social workers on Mr Littlemore's staff where they had continuously referred to 'Satanic abuse'. Councillor Kevin Hunt called for the Director to clarify his position.

"No one denied it when references were made to 'Satanic abuse' as late as Monday night. Quite frankly I am absolutely astonished that the Director is saying these things now."

Councillor Tony Heaford accused the Social Services of 'moving the goal posts'. The confusion surrounding the Rochdale case was further compounded a month later, at the end of October, when it transpired that the parents had not even been officially told of the allegations against them. In the six months since the dawn swoops, all their information had come from the media.

Amid all the confusion, I asked Matt Finnegan for his views on the affair, as he had followed the case closely, talking to social workers and parents alike during his reporting for the *Manchester Evening News*.

"Some of the things are horrific. One wonders why prosecutions have not been made. To my knowledge there has been no physical nor sexual abuse, but in some cases what has happened is not normal. Children may have been exposed to deviant practices."

Rochdale Social Services were further isolated when it was revealed that the Manchester branch of the Childwatch charity had been advising the parents. Judy Parry, area controller of Childwatch, stated that:

"Convicted criminals have been given more rights and support than these families."

This was in stark contrast to what Dianne Core, founder of Childwatch, reportedly said three months later:

"I am convinced that Satanic Abuse not only exists, but is a real danger to modern family life. About four thousand babies a year are born into covens to be used for sacrifices and cannibalism. This is only the tip of the iceberg."

Even before the full case had been heard at Manchester High Court, it was reported that the Social Services were planning to have ten of the children put up for legal adoption. One mother told reporters that if this happened: "I've got nothing left to live for. I might as well be dead."

Neighbours on the Langley council estate in Rochdale were more sensitive to the parents' plight, when the community decided to 'ban' Hallowe'en celebrations. At the beginning of December the hearing at Manchester High Court began, behind closed doors. It was estimated to last for about six weeks. In fact it took three months. The results were to be devastating for the proponents of the Satanic ritual abuse scenario.

In the weeks leading up to the outcome it must have been obvious to some which way the wind was blowing. Those in touch with social workers giving evidence must have formed a clear idea.

In February 1991, I telephoned Maureen Davies and asked for her views on Rochdale. It was a very subdued Ms Davies who told me she had no contact with the case, and therefore held no views on it. I then asked her who had provided the detailed background knowledge to social workers on black witchcraft and Satanic practices. She said she had no idea. When I suggested that Reachout had been instrumental in circularising information to social workers she made the following remark:

"I'm not with Reachout anymore. I operate on my own, dealing with those damaged by the occult. If you want to know anything else, then please phone Reachout in London."

She gave me a number and I dialled. A man answered the phone. When I asked him if Maureen Davies was still part of the Reachout organisation, he replied that she was, "but based in North Wales."

Mr Justice Douglas Brown took three days to sum up the Rochdale case - one for every month it had dragged on. By the close of Wednesday 7 March, it was all over.

'SATANIC RITUAL ABUSE' CHILDREN FREED BY JUDGE, was the lead story on the front page of *The Daily Telegraph*. SATAN QUIZ 'AMATEURS' headlined the *Manchester Evening News*, with a reference to Mr Justice Brown's conclusion on the unprofessionalism of the Social Services. The story made national newspaper headlines and featured heavily on networked television news programmes.

Mr Justice Brown said that social workers 'obsessive and mistaken' belief in Satanic ritual abuse had blinded them to the true facts, or rather lack of facts, of the case. They had accepted the bizarre statements of a six year-old retarded dyslexic boy as objective truth. They saw as insignificant the fact that he had been fed a ghastly diet of adult horror videos sometimes until one o'clock in the morning.

Of the original twenty children, aged between four and fourteen, six had already been returned to their parents. Of those remaining, the judge immediately released a further ten, with four remaining in care - their cases to be reviewed at a later date. The horror of the abduction of these children by the state was succinctly summed up in the editorial of *The Daily Telegraph*:

> We do not know whether any children were abused in Rochdale, but we do now know that what amounts to another form of child abuse took place - the abuse of being taken from one's parents and held for months by strangers.

Mr Justice Brown's criticisms ranged far and wide. Children had been given leading questions, and the initial interview with the six year-old had not been videotaped. Interviews which had been filmed were sometimes inaudible, and it was not possible to see the reaction on the children's faces. Anatomically correct dolls were used incorrectly, which may have prompted exaggeration and fabrication. Perhaps most damning of all was the admission that one of the leading social workers involved in the case had not read the recommendations in the Butler-Sloss report on the Cleveland debacle.

The social workers were not named by the judge. Their boss, Gordon Littlemore, did not get off so lightly. The day after the judgement, he resigned as Director of Rochdale's Social Services.

Who really was to blame? *The Mail On Sunday* had no doubts. They devoted six pages of their 10 March issue to the black farce. In a major article entitled; THE BRITISH INQUISITION, *The Mail* cited Maureen Davies and Reachout for being instrumental in importing the phenomenon from America. The paper claimed they had evidence that Ms Davies and other Christian fundamentalists had been involved in cases around the country where Satanic ritual abuse allegations had been made.

I fear the whole story will never really be told. Like Salem, a lot of innocent people were sucked into a vortex created by a belief that a network of black witches and Satanists were operating around the country. Like Salem, too, there may have been genuine supernatural elements somewhere in the equation. The parents of the six year-old boy who instigated the case in Rochdale, complained in 1985 of suffering poltergeist phenomena. The manifestations had only ceased after a priest had called and blessed the council house.

After Rochdale had finally been laid to rest, one would have thought that without evidence, there would be no more Satanic ritual abuse cases. But even as Mr Justice Brown was preparing his summing up, the whole ghastly cycle was set to start again. Nine children were taken from weeping parents by social workers on South Ronaldsay in the Orkney Islands, amongst accusations of ritualistic orgies.

Chapter Thirteen

SYMPATHY FOR THE DEVIL?

'GOD is My Father, and I BENEL am His Son. Thou shalt worship Him through Me to whom He gave dominion over the earth and all that is thereon. For I am the King of this world, and the Prince of Light and Darkness wherein all secrets are hid. I am the Father of thee My children. Therefore try Me not, nor test Me with thy will, for I shall taketh away his will that testeth Me. And I will destroy without mercy those that try to master Me.' The First Law of the Raz Kathab Mashal Scriptures

The Devil, Satan, Lucifer, Benel... His name is Legion for he is many.

But these names mean different things to different people. To the Christian fundamentalist Satan is a real supernatural entity slipping out of the underworld into this one in his battle for conquest. To the less orthodox Christian, the Devil is a state of mind, and although the concept epitomises evil, it is confined to individual thought and action, without objective existence. However, whether Satanism is an attitude of mind or the worship of a real dark fallen angel, both factions are certain of one thing; the Devil is the root of all paganism and its myriad permutations - including some other non-Christian religions too.

During the last two thousand years many competitive religious doctrines have been branded 'Satanic'. This is understandable. Christian fundamentalists are genuinely and utterly convinced that their god is *the* God. Logically, then, the gods of other peoples must be the Devil referred to in the New Testament.

The popular concept of Satanism is the practice and worship of things which are upside down, back to front, reversed, in the context of a Christian society. The Ten Commandments take on a new meaning when thou shalt becomes thou shalt not, and thou shalt not becomes thou shalt... Drunkenness, drug abuse, sacrifice and sexual perversion are the order of the day. The Dark God becomes the God of Light - it is *Alice Through The Looking Glass*, the insane logic of the mental asylum, it is the dark side of the moon...

Or is it ?

Certainly many religious groups have been persecuted for it. The Gnostics saw the world as profoundly evil - the true hell, and men were prisoners serving out a sentence. They decided that as the God of the Jews had created the Earth then He must be the true Satan. A good God would not put his subjects through so much misery. They regarded Jesus as an emissary from the good God, the bringer of enlightenment but not in essence human as this would place him in the domain of the god of the Old Testament who was the Devil.

This reverses the popular perception of the Hebrew Bible. Heroes become villains and villains become heroes. Moses is a persecutor of the Israelites and the serpent of Eden is a messenger from the good God bringing truth and knowledge to Adam and Eve, releasing them from the shackles of their creator.

These beliefs were transmitted to western Europe through the Bogomils and the Cathars, discussed in Chapter Two. If Yahweh was really the Devil, then the Ten Commandments were laws designed to keep people in subservience. One has to admit, that an objective reading of the Old Testament gives the impression of a deity who does not think twice about striking people dead, demands sacrifice in His honour, and indulges unsaintly emotions like jealousy and conceitedness.

In the Middle Ages, similar beliefs were expressed by the Waldensians, the Luciferians and the Knights Templar. Many of them paid for it with their lives.

That argument aside, evil is evil is evil. Torture, rape, murder, child abuse, ritual sacrifice - none of this is desirable in a fair and stable society. There is nothing uniquely 'Christian' about this attitude, it is just part of a larger blue-print for the survival of mankind as a sociological unit. Yet if we are to believe the Satanist commentators, these are the very things which the worshippers of the dark god practice.

But what do Satanists have to say for themselves ? What exactly is a 'Satanist'? I decided my researches had to extend beyond libraries and the private book collections of individuals. I wanted it straight from the horse's mouth. I wanted to meet a Satanist.

It was not easy. I made contact finally, but it was very difficult convincing this man of my objectivity. On one previous occasion he had bared all to the media, and, he claimed, paid the price with broken windows, death threats and an attack on his son. Only after counselling the views of someone known to us both did he agree to meet me at all. Even then it was not cut and dried. We spent the first hour sparring, as I impressed upon him my honest intent, and he dug here and there looking for flaws which would expose a cleverly contrived facade.

"I will tell you one thing," he said during this battle of wits. "I will tell you no lies. I cannot lie. That is one of our laws."

My straight-forward replies to his questions eventually paid off. Not only did he grant me the interview, but he also entrusted me with two hefty manuscripts, the results of twenty years work, which gave details of the sect's history and beliefs.

We went up into his study, and the interview began.

'Ramon Shareth' is no casual student of the occult. Of medium height, slim, with light grey hair curling up on the collar of his shirt, he is reminiscent of the late William Hartnell - the original Dr Who. Satanism is often viewed as the extreme end of the witchcraft spectrum, but what is the difference between it and Wicca ?

"Wicca is a blanket term for a lot of different types of groups. Anyone can take up witchcraft just by picking up a few books. They carry out a lot of their rituals naked - we're always robed. They put a lot into meaningless rituals, we read lessons, and six times a year a revision of all our Temples are carried out, incorporating any new laws or ideas to keep up with the times. There are fourteen meetings annually, we never carry out a ritual unless it is needed. Children are not allowed into the Temple under sixteen, although we have 'child dedication', similar to baptism. We don't believe in ramming our religion down anyone's throat.

"We don't recruit members - people come to us. Witches go to Spiritualist meetings to recruit because the people there are very susceptible. The basic Wiccan religion is nice. Trouble surfaces with everyone being autonomous - they make up their own rules and some of them incorporate orgies into their rituals. If they believe in it fervently enough, some witches develop real powers, then start using them. Some stay on the pagan path, others wander..."

My first surprise was to learn that there are two types of Satanists.

"We only use the term because that is what is accepted by people brought up on Hammer films and horror novels. What we believe is that the Satan mentioned in the Hebrew Bible, is the real Son of God - a prosecutor against evil, not evil itself. Satan is in fact the ruler of the Earth."

Proponents of this argument refer to the story of Christ's temptation in the wilderness, where Satan offered Him 'all the kingdoms of the world and the glory of them'; the inference being that these gifts are his to make. In St John's gospel the Devil is called 'the ruler of this world', and St Paul calls him 'the god of this world'. Then in St John 8, Jesus tells the Jews that their father is not God but the Devil.

In particular, Ramon referred to The Book Of Job:

> Now there was a day when the sons of God came to present themselves before the LORD, and Satan also came among them. The LORD said to Satan, "Whence have you come ?" Satan answered the LORD, "From going to and fro on the earth, and from walking up and down on it."

According to Ramon this passage tells us that God had several 'sons', and that Satan was one of them. This is repeated at the beginning of Job 2. Personally I find the wording ambiguous. It could mean that Satan was one of the sons of God, but it could also mean that when the sons gathered, Satan decided to gate-crash the party. However, the whole tone of the Book is one where Satan is allowed to test the faith of Job through various endurances. God holds up Job as a perfect subject, and Satan remarks that if Job was pushed far enough he would revolt. God thinks about that, then tells Satan to go ahead and check him out: "Behold, he is in your power; only spare his life."

Satan might not be the son of God, but some might presume that he is on God's payroll!

Benelists do not rely just on the Old Testament in their belief that Satan was the true son of God. In any case, they claim, the Hebrew Bible borrowed from earlier Sumerian scriptures. But what is in a name ? Quite a lot according to Ramon. This is what he says in his unpublished work *Orthodox Satanism/Benelism*:

> In the time of the first civilisation, the Sumerians had a plethora of gods. As time progressed they slowly reduced in number. So it came about that Bel-Enlil, who primarily was the God of the Air and Dispenser of Good and Retribution, became Lord of the World and the King of the Land and all its Regions. He was the

second in the Hierarchy of the Gods, and when the Mesopotamian Semites 'accepted' Him they adjusted His name from BeLeNLiL (the small letters denote that there were no vowels in their tongue) to BeNeL which means 'Son of God'. But when the Hebrews started to put together their own versions of theology, they changed His name to Satan and relegated Him to 'one of the sons of God', but even to them Satan only meant 'the adversary' and they prove in their scriptures that He only obeyed the commands of His Father, so He must have been a good Son, and 'the Adversary of Evil'.

"This is in opposition to 'Christian' Satanism which takes the Christian concept of Satan and then reverses Christian practices. Our religion is separate from Satanism as portrayed in the media or by Christianity. An analysis of both books of the Bible shows that in the New Testament God per se is referred to 50% less than in the Old Testament - in fact they've transposed the name of 'Jesus' for 'God'. The use of the name of 'Satan' has been increased by about 490% and his image changed from an obedient Son of God (Benel) to one of evil. References to 'devils' has also increased by 1,200%! Anything which was bad in the Hebrew Bible was called a 'devil'. Devils were only mentioned a few times. Christians have twisted the image of Satan, and also made it synonymous with 'the' Devil. They use this to bring people into the Christian and Moslem fold. It is used as a threat over people.

"We don't believe that Jesus was the son of God - if he existed at all. When the Romans conquered they took a census of the population. There's no record of any Jesus. There's Barabas and all the others but no Christ who claimed to be the Son of God and died on the cross. If he did exist, he was a man, practically unknown, perhaps a magician. You must realise that the New Testament was not written down until three hundred years after the alleged events. Then there were so many documents knocking around supposedly written by the disciples, that when the

New Testament was finally put together, more were thrown out than went in. As far as we're concerned, none of them were written by the disciples. Yet at the beginning it was a good religion, made for women and poor people. Up to then, women were not allowed to take a real part in religion, except as temple prostitutes and soothsayers. Although we don't accept the Christian scriptures as the word of God, there is occasionally some good writing in them. But most of this seems to be stolen off the Hindus anyway. For example, when the scriptures concerning the infancy of Jesus are compared to the two thousand years older Krishna writings, they are practically word for word translations."

But if you worship God, then why are your rituals based around Satan?

"God is the ruler of the universe and beyond, but he has sent his Son, Benel, and Astaroth, the Queen of Heaven, to take charge of things and watch over us. If we pray, we pray through Astaroth, and through Benel who have been sent to intercede on God's behalf.

"Let me put it another way. If you want to contact a publisher, you can't talk directly to the owner, you can't go to Maxwell, so you go through the editor to contact the Boss. Christians are supposed to go through Jesus, we go through Benel, Astaroth."

In the beginning, it was Ramon's quest for truth which took him on a journey both nefarious and rewarding. In 1942, at the age of fifteen, he joined the army as an apprentice technician. It was during these war years that he developed a yearning to become a Christian minister, and, according to him, was duly confirmed into the Church of England by the Archbishop of York.

"I wanted to be a missionary and go out and help people. Especially in poor countries. I didn't have the qualifications nor the education for it. When I asked my padre all the questions which were relevant to Christianity I got a knock back on everything I asked. It was 'God moves in mysterious ways', 'have faith'. This didn't suit me. I wanted answers. But when I started digging for answers I found all the wrong ones!"

He abandoned Christianity for good, and turned to paganism upon joining a 'white' witchcraft coven in Norfolk. But this practised 'idiotic and childish' rituals which disgusted him. He had similar experiences in Cumbria.

"These covens still exist. I had some terrible initiations. I've still got the scars on my back."

He left England for overseas service, and on his return met some Mormons, whom he thought were very good people. As he was keen to find a true religion he decided to join and was baptised by Elder Joseph Smith, namesake of the founder.

"And they were terrible."

After three years study for the Melchizedec Priesthood, he experienced a loss of freedom, and discovered most of their doctrine was just a sham.

"They are very good people in their own way, but when it comes to doing the things they preach, they're a failure. For instance, they talk about 'psychic healing', but they've never healed anyone as far as I know. I thought if there was a God who was supposed to look after people, help them develop their intelligence, make life happy, then why did none of these religions do that? They all seemed to make you sad, miserable - feel guilty at everything you did. I couldn't tolerate that.

"Eventually I found a group of Satanists based in Wales. They were about the worst of the lot! They did everything including hiring whores to dress up in rubber suits, kinky parties and wild sex orgies. They didn't give a damn as long as the money kept rolling in. It attracted a lot of people - especially in London. I thought, if this is Satanism, I don't want to be part of that either! But while I was there I obtained the confidence of the hierarchy, and got access to some very important documents and papers, which had a lot of truth in them. I had to transliterate a lot of them.

Our priesthood had its own set of characters similar to Sanskrit. It was in English but in Sanskrit, written right to left. I started searching out books on ancient religions. I found out there were things left out of the Bible. When I uncovered the origins of Christianity, I dug deeper. That was when I discovered the real thing..."

Like the Israelites who strayed while Moses was conversing with God on the top of Mount Sinai, the sect which Ramon had come upon bore little relationship to the one described in the original manuscripts. He was initiated into the 'Cultus Benelus', and after a short time was given the task of restructuring, returning it to the basic tenets of Benelism.

As he gathered together various secret grimoires and bibles, his position went from strength to strength until he was ready to totally reform the sect. When he acted a great number of members were expelled and all the Temples were disbanded, pending reorganisation.

Afterwards, the teachings and scriptures of Benel - or Satan - were set down in cohesive manuscript form under the directive of the 'Higher Benelic Conclave'.

How consistent has your 'religion' been down the years, I asked him?

"It's been consistent for centuries. It was an established religion in Great Britain, France, Germany and Italy, although they were known as 'Luciferians' up to the Reformation. We were not open because we were the first to be persecuted right until 1951. Then we were allowed to write about our beliefs for others to read. That was why our religion fell apart - there was little in writing and therefore no control."

What is your personal position now?

"That's a question I never answer. I'm not after kudos. In our Temples the most junior member is the senior. Everyone is that person's servant. The higher your status, the more a servant you become. I hold a powerful position through election by the Higher Council of Priests."

Over what area are you in control?

"Now you're trying to trap me!"

"No. It's a very relevant question. I'm interested, and my readers will be too."

Ramon stared ahead for a few seconds in contemplation.

"I co-ordinate the Temples across the country. The seventeen areas of the British Isles. Each has a Temple which is an area headquarters for many smaller 'circles'. These headquarters send in information to our central headquarters in Manchester. I don't control things, I co-ordinate; orchestrate. I ensure things are going right. But I do have the power of veto if necessary. Yet I have never exerted this power since our reformation in the fifties. I believe that all my Chief Priests should learn through consultation and have their say, do what the majority think is right."

How many members are there?

"My Chief Priests tell me there's between fifteen hundred and two thousand. But when I check the attendance notes I usually find there's just about half that in terms of the really faithful ones."

From what sort of backgrounds do your members come?

"Every walk of life - including some politicians. But we're interested in the person not their persona. We don't care whether they've got an education or not - whether they're rich or poor. As long as they are genuine, honest and sincere."

What of the Christian-Satanists? Do they outnumber you?

"I should say they do. But then not as one group. There is no 'network'. There are two groups here at the moment imported from America. Anton La Vey sent his troops over a while ago, and now we've got Michael Aquino."

But how genuine are they? How much of it is theatricals to entertain the media?

"I don't know. But there are a lot worse sects than them. A lot worse!"

Why is your network kept so secret?

"Some people are ignorant. Some people are stupid. They're willing to be persuaded that Satanism is evil. We don't want anything to do with Christian-Satanists. We don't have sex orgies, we don't allow the use of drugs or alcohol except for a drink during rituals."

What part does sex play in your rituals?

This question also elicited a negative reaction at first, because of a fear that any answer would be misquoted and taken out of context.

"In exactly the same way it does between you and your wife. Intercourse which takes place during rituals is done in private. It is only carried out as part of a ritual where energy is needed. Sexual energy is the most potent of all. However, it doesn't happen every night. If I told you that people leave our Temples because they don't get sex, you wouldn't believe me! But they do. Intercourse takes place at initiation and once annually from then on."

A lot of people are claiming that witchcraft and Satanism are linked with child abuse, animal and even human sacrifice.

"It's very hard to put these things right. If someone admits they've been dabbling in witchcraft or any aspect of occultism, and they've carried out any of these crimes, they are immediately dubbed 'Satanists'. Yet by the same logic, Christians who carry out the same crimes should be labelled as such in newspaper reports. That religion commits a minimum of four child murders every week in Great Britain. If newspapers were being fair they would carry headlines like: CHRISTIAN STARVES CHILD TO DEATH, JEWISH LANDLORD HARASSES TENANTS, CHRISTIAN JAILED FOR CHILD RAPE..."

But they would argue that the reason occultists are high-lighted is because perverted sex and sacrifice is attributed to pagan ritual.

"Christian-Satanists, maybe, but not us. Every religion is based around the utilisation of psychic energy. The more people gathered together the more energy is available to carry out work. Christians pray, occultists go into it in greater depth. They want physical, mental and sexual energy to work their 'magic'. At the moment I'm taking energy from you, the energy released by your brain. I may be able to use some of it later for something else."

Might I be taking your energy in also?

"I hope you are! That's what our teachings are based on - give and take. When it comes to child abuse and related activities, there is no energy at all in that, except expanded energy, wasted energy. When it comes to sacrifice - whether babies are sacrificed or not - that is a police matter. Certain so-called former witches who get their child sacrifice stories - unchecked - into the media, enjoy the notoriety.

"We don't do any of that because we don't need it. But Christian-Satanists do as they want; like vandals kicking car doors in. They must get some satisfaction out of it, even if psychologists cannot determine why. They like to kick against the Christian Church in this way, but the best way to kick against it is to ignore it. Although I don't expect anyone to believe me. They'll just say I'm covering up.

"Up to twenty years ago we used to sacrifice doves, ducks and hens, because in the old scriptures it states that sacrifices must be carried out on the altar. The idea is that you're giving up something for God. We found when it came to saving people who were dying it worked quite well. I would instruct a member of the Temple to procure a pair of pure white doves. This would not be an easy task. That person would have to expend a lot of time travelling from town to town, market place to market place. That was part of the sacrifice - their sacrifice. The birds would only be killed if they were part of a ritual to save someone who was dying. Then we discovered we could heal by releasing the doves. It worked out just as well because we had faith. We realised that God would help if we were doing the right thing."

There are various allegations that women are being impregnated then forced into abortions which are then used as sacrifices.

"You can blame Dennis Wheatley for that."

But is it happening?

"Not as far as I know. There was a person from Blackburn who claimed he had done that down at Stonehenge. But that's all."

But what about 'brood mares'?

"As I said before, people make these claims for notoriety."

But it is not notoriety if they don't want to be identified.

"Yes, but when it comes to making official statements they back down. I went with journalists from the *News of the World* to investigate reports in Newcastle of someone sacrificing children and drinking their blood. He claimed he was 'the most evil man in the world', but he was just another crank.

"I think the police should jump heavily on anyone making these claims. Let them use Gestapo methods or whatever is necessary to find the truth. They shouldn't be allowed to make such allegations with impunity."

Do you know anything about Derry Mainwaring Knight? He told his girlfriend he had sacrificed two children.

"None of our people down there had heard of him until the trial. There's no proof he was ever a Satanist, just a clever trickster."

What of the charges that occultists are not beyond using their powers to harm people?

"We prefer to carry out blessings. Blessings are easier, healing, helping people, and they work. Christians say it is evil to cast curses against someone. But if we find an evil person who is constantly doing bad, then we will do everything we can to stop them. But to do that we've got to isolate that person so no harm comes to anyone else. Sometimes it can be very, very difficult. And if too much energy was expended on cursing, and I was to lay my hands on someone who was ill, only for nothing to happen, I would feel awful."

How successful is this healing?

"We're very pleased with our success rate. We achieve things which sometimes make us sit back and think. About 80% of the people who approach us are completely cured. And remember, we are nearly always the last resort. We're the ones the afflicted turn to when the doctors and Christian priests have given up. But it can be very rewarding.

"A girl came to us recently with terrible pains in her stomach. We sent the pains away, but she said 'thanks for getting rid of my headache as well.' I said, 'what headache?' Apparently she had been suffering terrible pains in her head and neck for weeks. We didn't even know about that!

"We had a young man who came all the way up here from Devon. His back was so bad he couldn't move. He sat down and got stuck in the chair. I laid my hands on him and he was completely cured."

Ramon's face lit up as he related the story in obvious joy.

"He was ecstatic! Before, he couldn't even lift up his arms and put his own vest on. Now he kept lifting up his arms and grinning. It was the first time he had been able to do this in eight years!"

One of the explanations for psychic healing is that it is psychosomatic, mind over matter. They expect to be cured so they are, usually only temporarily.

"You're dead right. And we don't make claims to the contrary. If it cures them and takes away the pain - fine. It doesn't matter what they think or what we think as long as it works. But we're certain this isn't the explanation in most of our cases, and it does not account for 'absent healing'. We have had friends and relatives of seriously ill or dying people coming to us for help. We will carry out a ritual and cure that person without them knowing what we have done. That proves there is something external at work."

During rituals members of The Orthodox Temple of the Prince wear long black robes with wide sleeves. Originally hoods with slitted eyes were also worn, although rarely nowadays, Ramon told me. This in itself evokes stock images of evil in most peoples minds, and why 'black'? *Orthodox Satanism/Benelism* has an explanation:

Black is probably the most abundant 'colour' in the world. To us darkness represents what is hidden, the mysterious. Nearly all people are frightened of the unknown, the solution therefore is knowledge, and once gained they will have passed through the Abyss into the light and nothing should be hidden from them. They will have no fears, and when there is no fear there is no hesitation, no floundering. We are successful in what we do because everything is clear to us, we SEE THE LIGHT. It is also well known that black is curative, for nature heals at night. Scientifically, black absorbs colours which are vibrations. This should tell you why we wear black robes, for by so doing we absorb all the vibrations which are given out during the meeting, hence our teachings on Endemic Spiritual and Sexual Osmosis which is the essence of our meetings and rituals. In most countries the very dark colours are considered to be spiritual.

In his answer, Ramon revealed a more prosaic reason.

"We wear black robes because what is beneath remains a secret. It is your own private temple. If someone does decide to disrobe then that person has made a conscious decision to show everyone their personal temple. Then they are sacrificing themselves to us. Black robes also make everyone equal. Imagine how a girl might feel if the woman next to her was wearing a diamantee dress, while she could only afford a frock from

Woolworth. She might have twice the intelligence, but appearances would deceive. We know what women feel - we know what men feel. In black robes everyone is the same."

One of the main rituals performed by the Benelists is the black mass. Long held to be the antithesis of the Christian mass, and practised as such by what Ramon terms 'Christian-Satanists', they give an altogether different interpretation.

They believe the title was invented by 'the inquisitional Christians' during the Middle Ages, and was adopted by the Luciferian German council not long afterwards, who attached it to their Rite of the Dead. The black mass added to the existing ritual a dimension of prayers to all those 'cruelly tortured and murdered by the Christians'. Ramon also pointed out that their black mass is performed on a Satanist altar, at the most once a year, and not on a Christian one. Although this explanation seems plausible, I cannot help feeling they are being deliberately controversial. Why call it the 'black mass' at all?

During the mass the 'most beautiful and sincere member' of the Temple is led robed towards the 'Major Altar' where she agrees to become 'Queen of the Sabbat'. She then disrobes and is symbolically washed, prostrate on the altar. The Presiding Priest steps forward, reads out a 'homage', then lays his hand on her whereupon she 'dies', 'representing all the souls murdered by the Christians over the centuries'.

The 'Altar Priestess' then pours wine into a chalice and it is placed on the naked girl's stomach, where it is 'charged with life' and the 'blessings of the Prince', and a plea of reincarnation is made for all the 'murdered' souls. The Presiding Priest and the rest of the Circle then taste the wine, and finally recite an invocation:

"We ask our Prince to bless all those, both followers and others, who were tortured, suffered and died through the greed and murderous practices of those who opposed us during the dark period of our history. May those martyrs find peace and happiness in their new lives, for they shall always be remembered during this Mass which has been named for them; The black mass. Amen."

It took several visits before Ramon had enough trust and confidence in me to allow me access to his Temple. At the entrance I was instructed to remove my shoes, as the Temple floor was deemed 'holy ground'.

The atmosphere was sombre and peaceful, heavy with expectation. There was a table in one corner decorated with occult symbols and seating around the walls, but the focus of the room was the Satanic altar. Black velvet drapes adorned it, framing the chalices, wine flagons and ceremonial daggers, used during rituals including the black mass.

I imagined the naked figure of the Queen of the Sabbat prostrate on this altar, saw the Temple members, robed, standing before her vulnerability, heard Ramon Shareth, Presiding Priest, invoke the mass in the name of the Prince.

Ramon made it clear that there was more to the black mass than is detailed in his book, more than he was prepared to make public.

"But there is no 'orgy' or other devious practices omitted," he added hastily.

What of other rituals? Does his sect carry out rituals to invoke 'demons'?

"Not at all. The idea of demons existing in other dimensions is utter nonsense. The only demons which exist are those inside a person's heart. 'Demonic' is a graphic way of describing certain behaviour."

If you don't believe in supernatural entities, where does that leave Satan?

"Benel is a force, a personality. That's why we don't have portraits of Him in our Temples and Circles. We do have portraits of Astaroth, to make it easier to differentiate between the two.

You could picture Benel as looking like a Greek god if it helps you focus your thoughts."

Nevertheless, most Christians believe that demons have an independent existence, that they are the servants of Satan.

"They would wouldn't they ? They believe that Satan exists with horns, cloven feet and a tail. But to us the Christian-Satan figure is the same as their demons - attitudes of mind. If a Christian does something evil they say 'the Devil has got into him'. This is merely an abdication of responsibility for one's own actions. A hook to hang all their kinks on. Devils!

"All this trouble has only surfaced in the last few years. Before that we co-existed with little trouble. I was close friends with a Catholic priest. When his church was demolished he presented me with the beautiful leather-bound Bible used during services. It is one of my most treasured possessions. It's wrong that these people should be persecuting us again."

Chapter Fourteen

ABROAD

Abroad is unutterably bloody and foreigners are fiends.
Nancy Mitford

It will come as no surprise to learn that witchcraft abroad, particularly in America, parallels the British experience. Maureen Davies has contacts in the USA, South Africa and Australia, and told me "the same sort of situation" exists in those places as in Britain.

The witchcraft controversy started getting a breezy public airing in America at the beginning of the eighties; several years before it really took off here. This was about the same time we started hearing of showbiz Christian evangelists Swaggart and Bakker. They injected a heady religious fervour into their shows not seen in decades. Both men have since fallen from grace, the former from revelations of fornicating with a prostitute; and the latter from charges of fraud. They were responsible for creating an atmosphere of competition between ministries to attract the most converts. The bigger the headlines the bigger the congregation. Chat show host, Geraldo Rivera was instrumental in bringing to everyone's attention alleged ritual sexual abuse of children. This was reinforced by a book called *Michelle Remembers*, written by Michelle Smith and Lawrence Pazder. It is a record of a Canadian woman's detailed confession to her psychiatrist of how she was allegedly abused by Satanists as a child. The book has come in for a lot of criticism. Reading it, one can understand why.

Michelle, married and in her late twenties, had already seen Dr Pazder several years earlier for trauma connected with her upbringing. Her father was a violent drunk who disappeared for months on end. In 1976, Michele went back to see her psychiatrist after a nightmare connected with a miscarriage. Michelle was certain that there was a huge blockage in her mind holding back something terrible which had happened when she was five years old. Over the next fourteen months, the repressed 'memories' emerged, consecutively, paralleling the alleged events of twenty two years before. When Michelle entered this twilight zone of altered consciousness, it was as if she had travelled back in time.

The young woman spoke in the voice of a five year-old, her narration accompanied by screaming and tears. She described in detail how her mother had given her up to a temple of Satanists for preparation for use in a ritual called The Feast Of The Beast. The child was subjected to physical, sexual and psychological abuse in an attempt to strip her of all humanity, to convince her that no-one loved her, and that she was undeserving of love.

She was locked up for a time in the cellar of a deserted house, living in her own filth. Later she was transferred to the temple itself where she was forced to witness the sacrifice of foetuses, the sexual abuse of other children and ritual murder. Snakes were used to sexually abuse her. Michelle was kept in a cage on meagre rations, forced to take part in perverted rituals, her gaolers being nice one moment, then hideous the next, in a concerted effort to destroy her spirit. Similar motifs were destined to emerge several years later, as we have seen, in Satanic ritual abuse cases across Britain.

Reading the book, one cannot help feeling that Dr Pazder is not as objective as he might be. Indeed, the doctor/patient relationship is illustrated as going far beyond the norm when

Pazder leaves the young woman a note on his tape recorder, referring to his feelings for her:

It is not natural, social, hospitable, or sexual. It is not the feeling of children for parents or vice versa. It is not brotherly love. It is not the love for a female. It is beyond all my reasoning and beyond all that I can specifically say. Some inexplicable power of destiny that brought about our union. It is one soul with two bodies...

The quote was from Montaigne, written at the time of those other witch hunts.

Although the psychiatrist, and even Michelle, occasionally speculate on the objective reality of her 'memories', Dr Pazder on the whole seems convinced of their authenticity. He encourages this belief with the traumatised young woman, thus reinforcing the whole diabolical scenario. Even Dr Pazder pauses to reassess his views when Michelle describes how Satan himself eventually materialises out of the flames of the temple fire...

It is interesting how Michelle's 'repressed memories' seem in perfect accordance with Catholic dogma. Pazder himself is a Catholic, and, at Michelle's request, she was introduced to three priests, one of them, Father Guy, early on in the investigation. Before the experience was through, Michelle herself was baptised into the faith.

It does not surprise critics, then, that the Virgin Mary appeared to the five year-old Michelle to help her fight against Satan, with Christ, visible, but taking a back seat. There is also a series of photographs taken by Dr Pazder during the burning of a bench decorated with occult symbols. Father Guy supervised the fire ceremony. In the pictures is an unidentifiable image which 'moves' across from the priest to Michelle. The mysterious image, although vague, is interpreted as the Virgin Mary holding the baby Jesus.

When Pazder tries to check out parts of Michelle's story, the results are sometimes intriguing, but always ambiguous. More concrete are the rashes and marks which appeared on her body during the clinical sessions. These marks have been graphically photographed. Dr Pazder refers to them as 'body memories', as if they are a replay of the results of actual physical abuse - which, of course, they may be. However, parapsychologists have known for years of the power of the mind to alter the body - most vividly illustrated in the phenomenon of stigmata.

There is plentiful documentary proof of individuals who have borne the bloody wounds of Christ, yet no-one would suggest that at one time these stigmatics were nailed to a cross! On Michelle appeared a trowel-like bruise on her neck. This was equated with part of the narrative where Michelle describes Satan's tail wrapping itself about her neck.

Needless to say, the child defeats Satan and his followers, and is returned to her mother. The most bemusing part of the case for me is Michelle's attitude towards her mother who later died of cancer when the girl was in her teens. Even though her father was a tyrant, before the revelations Michelle thought she had always had a loving relationship with Mrs Smith. Yet the story which emerges during those fourteen months depicts the woman as an uncaring beastly inhuman entity who stood by and observed the torture of her little girl.

Typical of the resultant confusion was an article by John Crewdson and published in the *Chicago Tribune* of 29 July 1985, entitled; SATANISM HAUNTS TALES OF CHILD SEX ABUSE. Here is an extract:

> Scores of children in more than half a dozen California communities are telling authorities that they have been sexually abused by groups of adults who also forced them to take part in Satanic-type rituals, including the drinking of blood, cannibalism, and the sacrificial murders of other children.
>
> Last month deputy sheriffs in Toledo dug up acres of suburban fields after receiving a tip that a local Satanic cult had buried as many as 75 bodies in the area. No bodies were found.

In Mendocino County, north of San Francisco, several children who attended the same pre-school have told police they were made to chant "Baby Jesus is dead" and subjected to other Satanic rituals as a prelude to being sexually abused.

Despite the lack of evidence, various psychiatrists and social workers were convinced the children were telling the truth:

"It's something I don't want to be identified as knowing that much about," said a psychiatrist who has interviewed the children in one of the cases. "I think anybody who works in this area ought to carry a badge and wear a gun. And not have a family."

"Good luck with your life," said another child therapist, one of whose patients is among the children making such accusations. "My car was blown up 10 days ago."

The first therapist, who said he had heard sexually abused children speak of "eating flesh, being forced to kill other children, things like that," had initially been sceptical of the children's accounts.

But there was an inbuilt danger in the authorities promoting these stories. A jury might be able to make a balanced decision based purely on child abuse allegations, but the Satanic angle to most was pure fantasy; a situation British police were to warn of several years later. In one case where a nine year-old girl was accusing her natural father, involved with a Satanic cult, of abusing her, a mistrial was announced when the jury became deadlocked. It was the occult details of her suffering which sowed confusion in the minds of the jurors.

Hal Jewitt, deputy district attorney in Contra Costa County, and the girl's psychotherapist, told Crewdson this:

"There's no doubt in my mind that she was a participant in Satanic worship. She also described incidents of human sacrifice, bestiality and cannibalism, how her father put his hand around her hand and then the two of them plunged a knife into the chest of an infant. That raises some questions."

The psychotheraphist harbours no such doubts: "Her description of how the guts pop out when you slit open a live abdomen does justice to a Vietnam War veteran."

Things are always more extreme in America. Satanist, Charles Manson and his followers, started the ball rolling with the ritual slaying of beautiful Sharon Tate and six others on 9 August 1969, in California. The star was eight months pregnant. Since then others have emerged from the dark recesses of witchcraft's many mansions. Maury Terry, author of *The Ultimate Evil*, claims that there is a network of Satanic cults at work across America, responsible for the Manson killings, and for the 'Son of Sam' slayings in New York. At the time, it was alleged that one man, David Berkowitz, was responsible for all the 'Son of Sam' killings, when victims, usually pretty girls, were gunned down at point blank range. Maury, an investigative journalist, and others uncovered over a period of years the fact that Berkowitz belonged to a Satanic cult. Several cult members had carried out the murders, which had ritual significance. Latest of these ritual murderers is Richard Ramirez, the 'Night Stalker' who terrorised Southern California between 1984 and 1985.

During the trial in October 1989, it was proven that he was responsible for at least thirteen ritual killings. Victims were shot, raped, sexually abused, and occult symbols were carved into their bodies. Ramirez was unrepentant in the court, and smirked as relatives wept. He was sent to the gas chamber, but the American appeal procedure could mean he might drag out the misery a further six years before sentence is carried out. In that time the Texan drifter might well become a media star. Juror Donald McGee told reporter Tony Brenna:

"I've spent time in the services. I've seen dead bodies before. But the pictures they showed us here of what this man has done turned my guts. Even now I can't sleep nights, and I know there are other jurors who remain horrified by the images that have been presented in photographs and testimony."

Diabolical killings, as we have all ready seen, are not confined to the United States. *The Daily Mirror* of 23 October 1989 carried one of those over-saturated headlines peculiar to newspaper editors: BLOOD-DRINKING SATAN GIRLS IN MURDER ORGY. The story, by Coral O'Connor, was from Brisbane, Australia.

According to the report, four young women cruised around the city in a car looking for a victim. They found forty seven year-old council employee, Edward Baldock, who had been drinking in a club. They abducted the man and took him to a lover's lane where he was hacked to death. His mutilated body was later found by a jogger. Why the ritual killing took place is unsure, although a police officer commented about one of the killers: "One has existed on nothing else but animal blood for the past week." The trial ended on 15 February 1991, with two women sent down for life, another for eight years, and one acquitted.

Horror stories aside, witchcraft exists in Australia and America in its pagan guise without drawing quite as many punches. Indeed, in the USA it is becoming fairly institutionalised. After the witchcraft resurrection in Britain, the craft was reintroduced into America. Occult writers Sybil Leek and Raymond Buckland helped popularise it. Mrs Leek, an English clairvoyant with a coven in the New Forest, went to the USA originally to lecture, and decided to stay. The lack of a state religion meant there was no natural adversary, and Wicca flourished. This 'neo-pagan explosion' has in the eyes of some British witches 'outshone the amateur shambolic organisation in Europe'. American witches are legally registered, have tax-free status and can perform marriages. Unlike their European counterparts who meet in temporary secret places, they have buildings specifically for the purpose. When British witch, Barbara Brandolani, tried to purchase a derelict church for use as a pagan centre several years ago, she received neither financial nor moral support from other occultists. Such is the organisation across the Atlantic pond, there even exists a federation of Wicca churches.

One group have bought a two hundred acre nature reserve in Wisconsin, where they grow herbs, celebrate sabbats, meditate and carry out healing. High Priestess of the Circle Sanctuary, Selina Fox, told the Farrars they were up against a strong Christian movement who painted Wicca as Satanic. This is what Ms Fox said in *The Life And Times Of A Modern Witch*:

> Despite these advances, the struggle for pagan religious freedom is far from over. Some preachers, claiming to be Christian, have been falsely calling the Craft Devil Worship and evil, and have been actively urging their flocks to do some very unChristian-like things, such as to hate, persecute and even kill witches.

In Autumn of 1985, legislation was proposed in Washington to take away church status from Wiccan covens, but after thousands of witches protested nationwide, it was dropped. Many Americans who are not occultists take an active part in Hallowe'en celebrations.

The Guardian of 31 October 1989 reported that the American costume industry expected a four hundred million dollar boost from Hallowe'en that year. Mr Matt Goldberg of the Topstone Costume Company said that 85% of his business was from adults. Five years earlier, threats of razor blades in apples and poisoned sweets had taken children off the streets and their parents had become more involved at home.

Maureen Davies on her return from a fact-finding mission to the United States, told me:

"I went to see how the Churches were dealing with the witchcraft problem. The system in America is very different. The counselling of individuals by the various agencies is done within psychological dimensions. I was saddened really by the way they were dealing with it. They were trying to humanise a problem which is spiritual. It was sad to see some of the diagnoses placed on these individuals. I came back home more encouraged by the way we were doing things, even though we were behind them in introducing the problem to Britain. We are working with the police, social workers - and it's good to see. We're not on top of the situation, but there is a real awareness of what is happening."

Sandi Gallant of the Intelligence Division of the San Francisco Police Department, is considered a leading authority on occult crime, and has lectured widely. She is convinced that a number of homicides perceived as normal murders, are in fact ritual deaths not recognised as such because police officers are ignorant of the signs. Some people are sceptical, however, and others think she has gone too far. In 1988, she visited Britain to advise 'witchfinders' of her techniques, and we have seen the results...

Despite all this, Wiccan groups are firmly established in the United States, along with other occult groups. There are two principal Satanist organisations. Both the Temple of Set and the Church of Satan are headquartered in San Francisco.

We have met Michael Aquino, High Priest of the Temple of Set, in a previous chapter. 'Set' is an Egyptian god, identified with Satan, who instructed black magicians in the techniques of sorcery. Aquino is in fact an Army Lieutenant Colonel in St Louis, formerly stationed in San Francisco. It was there that he and his wife were linked with child molestation, although they were not charged with any crime. Aquino puts it down to 'religious bigotry'. Both groups deny any kind of criminal activity, and Sandi Gallant admits there is no proof to the contrary.

The Temple of Set was in fact set up by a splinter group who left the Church of Satan in 1975, after accusing leader La Vey of selling out to the media.

The theatrical Anton Szandor La Vey, a former circus artist and police photographer, founded the Church of Satan in 1966. He calls himself 'The Black Pope', and has dedicated the last twenty four years of his life to glorifying all carnal pleasures. The estimated 25,000 members of the Church take part in black masses conducted over naked women, baptisms, weddings and funerals based on ceremonies from La Vey's own Satanic Bible. Apart from America, it is claimed that churches have been established in England, France, Germany, Australia and Africa.

Ironically, La Vey played the part of the Devil in Polanski's classic film *Rosemary's Baby*, released in 1968. It told the chillingly executed story of a young woman tricked into giving birth to the Devil's son. Ironic, because it was the following year that the Manson gang butchered Polanski's own pregnant wife in the name of Satan.

Chapter Fifteen

CONFESSION

What was he doing the great god Pan
Down in the reeds by the river ?
Spreading ruin and scattering ban,
Splashing and paddling with hoofs of a goat,
And breaking the golden lilies afloat
With the dragon-fly on the river.
Elizabeth Barrett Browning

The small boy adjusted his stetson, buckled his gun belt and went outside to join his friends. There was to be a gun fight on Nelson Road.

The road was wide, quiet, tree-lined, and to a boy of five, seemed to go on forever... At the top of the road, the group of similarly dressed youngsters split into two. One half galloped off along the pavement slapping their backsides as they went, while the others remained where they were, waiting for their friends to get into position. Finally, the posse started to hunt the outlaws who had galloped away - spoiling for a fight.

The boys, armed with imitation revolvers and rifles loaded with explosive caps, darted between driveways, from behind stone walls and low hedges until the two groups caught sight of one another. Suddenly, battle commenced.

It rampaged down Nelson Road, the trespass rights of house-holders blatantly ignored, as boys fell dead and wounded only to miraculously rise again to fire off another round. Suddenly the noise, the bedlam, stopped. Several of the boys had noticed something in a house nearby. Silently, the others fell into line.

Standing in the large bay window of the house was a woman. This was 1959, but even then she was an anachronism. The woman was tall and swathed in layers of clothing. A shawl covered the top part of her head, draped across her shoulders. Her hair, the colour of sun-bleached straw, was woven into plaits which twisted down over her chest almost to her waist. But the face which peered out from this silvery halo was heavily lined and the chin square and protruding. From the fluted sleeves projected hands which were large and boney. She could have been plucked from a Hans Christian Andersen fairy story.

This strange apparition which had so abruptly stopped the children in play now smiled queerly, and the left hand moved slowly up and down in the parody of a wave. Was she waving or beckoning, the small boy in the stetson wondered? Either way he felt the tentacles of fear reach out and clutch at his tummy.

Suddenly the enchantment was broken.

"Witch! Witch!" A piping voice cried. "She's a Witch!" Most of the other boys joined in.

Then they did what small boys do when they are in a group and afraid. They made a lot of noise, jumped up and down like chimpanzees and stuck their tongues out defiantly. Except for the boy in the stetson. He watched as a second woman appeared at the window, dressed much like the first, and with an angry sideways glance at the assembled menagerie, took the other's arm and turned her away, back into the shadows of the room. He watched, then went home, those tentacles of fear still squeezing uncomfortably the entrails of his stomach.

Back in the late fifties that stetson and gun belt were constant companions during most of my leisure time out of school. But then nearly every boy was cowboy crazy in those days. Yet even though my heroes were Roy Rogers and the Lone Ranger, I also knew how to recognise a witch when I saw one. I lost no time in telling my mother about the witch who lived near the bottom of Nelson Road. This one must be the wicked witch, I conjectured, or the Gingerbread House witch, because hadn't she tried to entice us into her home? Didn't witches eat small children?

My mother was annoyed, not with the witch for frightening us but with our behaviour. She sat me down and very patiently explained why we were wrong.

Of course, the woman was not a witch. She was mentally retarded and that slow waving and crooked smile was the small child within trying to control that cumbersome grown-up body in an attempt to communicate with us. She must have heard the noisy sound of other children playing and wanted to join in. She was waving to us, and instead of a returning smile, she received an exhibition of ignorance and fear. No wonder her sister looked so angry. A part of the shame I felt then has remained with me to this day.

Needless to say, there is a very important lesson here. Many innocent people like my 'witch' were put to death on the say-so of children. That is the trouble when people group together in a 'society'. Often the mob rules and crass intolerance emerges towards eccentrics and minority thinkers who refuse to run with the herd, not to mention those with mental deficiencies.

'Extremism' is a dirty word. Excess is too much of anything. Even a surfeit of love can smother a child. It seems that most things are okay in moderation. Especially religion. Moderation comes in gentle streams. It allows us to take in things in a leisurely way, examine and modify them, separate the facts from the fantasy. When belief overtakes reason the rampaging monster of intolerance rears its head and begins to snort and dig its hoofs in. Before you know what is coming, it begins to charge, kicking out in every direction. It does not care. It has lost its reason. The good fall with the bad.

Is this what has happened in the Satanic ritual abuse cases? Have social workers been persuaded into something which has little, if any, foundation in fact? Is it all down to hysteria and the contents of horror videos that young minds have been unable to handle? Latest of these occurred in the Orkney Isles, where social workers and police took away nine children from families on South Ronaldsay, together, according to *Today*, with cloaks, hoods, masks and books.

The children were taken from their parents the week before Mr Justice Brown gave his summing up on the Rochdale case. Parents were filmed in obvious distress. Other villagers told reporters it was Cleveland again, the Salem witch hunt revisited. One wonders if Mr Justice Brown's judgement had been the week before, whether the abductions would have taken place. By then it was too late - the state machinery had been set in motion.

It was alleged by social workers that a coven of witches operated on the island. During rituals, a local priest stood at the centre of a circle formed of coven members and children. He held a shepherd's crook. As they danced around the priest to 'ritualistic' music, the cleric snatched the children, one at a time, into the circle, where he allegedly abused them. Afterwards an orgy took place between adults, and children and adults.

The priest was interviewed on television. He asked the interviewer if he thought an elderly clergyman with a heart condition would be capable of such a thing. Sue Miller, Team Leader of the social workers, was unrepentant...

Predictably, by now, the witchcraft allegations were judged to be without foundation, and a tearful reunion took place between parents and their off-spring on 4 April.

Sheriff David Kelbie said the social workers' case was "fundamentally flawed". He said that the children had been taken from their parents and "subjected to cross-examination designed to break them down and make them admit to being abused." He blamed one social worker in particular, Gordon Sloan, the

Reporter to the children's panel, who, the Sheriff said, failed to carry out procedures according to the law. In Scottish law, the Reporter is responsible for investigating cases, collecting evidence and deciding whether or not the case should go before a panel. Mr Sloan's predecessor, a Mrs Katherine Kemp, was suspended in April 1990 for publicly criticising the social work department for its running of a children's home. She was later vindicated. Many of the Orkney parents were convinced Mrs Kemp would have handled their cases differently. She has now been reinstated.

According to the *Daily Mail* of 5 April, Maureen Davies lectured at a seminar on Satanism in November 1990 in Aberdeen. Two Orkney social workers attended.

One wonders afresh at these detailed 'eye-witness' accounts from children and adults. These people are so convinced, the adults in particular, such as Michelle Smith, Audrey Harper and 'Sarah', who believes she has been abducted regularly by Satanists. One is also reminded of Isobel Gowdie. Yet there is no concrete evidence for these allegations. Are we dealing with an unrecognised phenomenon that straddles the no-man's land between 'fantasy' and 'reality'? Something which is not quite one, and not quite the other?

There is a similarity here with another line of research I have been involved in for a number of years with the assistance of mental health specialists - that of UFO abductions.

There are now hundreds of documented cases from around the world of individuals who have experienced a UFO abduction. Briefly, an individual - or sometimes a group of people - have a UFO sighting, after which they cannot account for a period of time, usually between one and two hours. Over the course of weeks, months, or even years, the witnesses start to have terrible nightmares in which they are inside a 'spacecraft', fastened down on a table and examined by 'aliens'. Sometimes hypnotic regression is used. During this, the witness is taken back to the date of the experience, where he 're-lives' it. This method seems to be a short cut through the gradual leaching out of repressed 'memories' via dreams and nightmares.

The vast majority of abductees lead normal, rational lives, except for the irrationality of the experience. Most of them are bewildered and sometimes afraid. Those who have been psychologically tested come out of it with flying colours.

There are a number of parallels here with the detailed accounts given by alleged Satanic abuse victims. The 'temple' equates with the dome-shaped room of the 'spacecraft'. In one there is an altar upon which abuse and human sacrifice takes place, in the other, the abductee is restrained on a 'table' and examined by non-human entities. Individuals are taken to these locations against their will. Witchcraft experientialists claim they were originally abused as very young children and now fear for their own off-spring. UFO abductees often discover as they re-examine incidents in their childhood, that the 'aliens' have regularly taken them away for examination, and now it is happening to their own children. These incidents have, they believe, been buried deep in their subconsciousness, and a screen memory substituted instead. Furthermore, American ufologists have uncovered hidden 'memories' in female abductees of being impregnated by aliens, who re-abduct them months later for removal of the fully formed hybrid, just as certain women believe that they have been made pregnant by Satanists, who later abort the foetus for use in black magic rituals.

In both cases, psychologists and psychiatrists have gone on record stating that in their opinion, the subjects have undergone real objective experiences. In both areas hard evidence has been lacking - yet both groups are convinced of the reality of the phenomenon.

A straight psychological answer seems too simplistic. Certainly there is a degree of psychological abnormality involved - we seem to be dealing with different aspects of a root phenomenon - it is psychology plus ingredient 'X'. Perhaps we are dealing with an objective phenomenon which affects percipients subjectively.

The Christian fundamentalist movement is having some success in stemming the tide of witchcraft, even in its milder forms. The Church Society put pressure on Dr Robert Runcie, accusing him of bringing paganism into Christianity, when the Church of England planned a multifaith festival of the environment at Canterbury Cathedral in September 1989. According to *The Guardian*, the ceremony was toned down. The Reverend Robert Vaughan came in for criticism when he brought forward Holy Communion on 11 September 1989 to accommodate the pagan festival of the Horn Dance in the village of Abbots Bromley. The dance starts at 8am and ends at dusk. Six men carrying reindeer horns of an unknown age, perform the ritual dance at the vicarage, the manor house and in the village. The ritual is centuries old.

A phenomenon which has emerged in recent years is that of the Psychic Fair. It is a little reminiscent of fairs of old which roved from village to village. These fairs usually take place in hotels and municipal halls. They are composed of mediums offering astrology charts, palmistry and tarot card readings, dealers selling charms and occult paraphernalia, books on esoteric religions and psychic healers. Some organisers are making a lot of money from them. They attract the curious, the converted and those just out for a bit of fun.

The Church has kicked up such a fuss that most local newspapers do not even mention them now. The Church does not see why the Devil should receive free publicity in 'our' press. To a local paper faced with late night pub fights and lost pet stories, Psychic Fairs are news but they might just as well not exist.

The 5 August 1989 edition of *Psychic News* carries an item headed; HOTELS IMPOSE BAN ON ANY FURTHER PSYCHIC FESTIVALS. This is what it said in essence:

Though more than 150 people attended a Psychics and Mystics meeting in Lynn, Norfolk, last month, two hotels have banned future events. The psychics and mystics event was held at the Duke's Head Hotel. Its banqueting manager, David Hurst, told a reporter the booking was "a mistake" which would not be repeated. The gathering was the third in four months to take place in Lynn.

Previously two were held at the Globe Hotel. Manager Dave Davies commented, "The psychics are not welcome here." some of his staff "were unnerved and disturbed by these people being here," Mr Davies continued.

"I had a lot of complaints. It was a mistake to accept the booking. Never again !"

Local clergy fuelled the situation by claiming the meetings could be dangerous and lead to the unsuspecting being lured into black magic, occultism and witchcraft.

Canon Michael Yorke of St Margaret's Church expressed his views. "The boundary line between spiritual disturbance and mental disturbance is very fine. This sort of thing can lead people into great confusion and into the occults. In general," he alleged, "it is full of fraud."

"Unchristian" was the term used by the Rev Patrick Ryley of St John the Evangelist Church. "It is something we've got to guard against."

The event's organiser, Margaret Pickering, said attendances were increasing with every one put on.

"People come to us because what we do is natural. the Church claims that we manipulate people - but that is what it is doing. It manipulates the masses."

On 18 April, Trust House Forte, the largest group of hotels and exhibition halls in the United Kingdom, announced a ban on further Psychic Fairs on their properties. An event planned at Haigh Hall in Lancashire for January 1990 was scrapped after local churches put pressure on Wigan council. Things took a personal turn when I read a report from the publishers of a previous book of mine.

A rep had called into a bookshop in Birmingham and enquired why they had refused to stock my book. The manager replied that they stocked nothing connected with the 'occult' as there 'was no demand'. When the rep showed surprise, the manager admitted that the real reason was because of pressure from local Christian groups. The book concerned was critical of claims of certain mysterious deaths which had been linked with alleged paranormal causes. Despite its title, *Death By Supernatural Causes?* was not about the occult at all!

Never judge a book by its cover, says the old adage, but that is exactly what is happening. Fundamentalist and evangelical pressure groups are having a detrimental effect on the right of an author to be read. Salman Rushdie is not the only victim of religious extremism. Sarah Strickland and Rosie Waterhouse of *The Independent On Sunday* have reported on many other examples.

Despite protestations, Walker Books changed the title of Teresa Tomlinson's book, *Summer Witches*, to *The Secret Place*, after a book club made it a condition of placing a large order. Another children's author, Helen Cresswell, said she had been warned by school heads not to mention the word 'witch' during workshop activities. The superb BBC serialisation of her novel, *Moondial*, caused a howl of protest from fundamentalists. Some of the letters received from Christians were so upsetting, the Head of Children's Programmes could not show them to Ms Cresswell. Puffin said it had received complaints about its Hallowe'en promotion of several old and new books.

Despite all this, the veteran children's BBC television programme, *Blue Peter*, fought back against critics who said Hallowe'en should be banned. In an edition transmitted live on 26 October 1989, and repeated the following Sunday, most of the programme was dedicated to Hallowe'en celebrations. At the close, presenter John Leslie made this statement:

"We think Hallowe'en is just a bit of fun. If anyone tries to tell you any different, ignore them - its rubbish!"

Where does this leave us? Is it all rubbish? I fear not. In the closing weeks of 1989 came a report of a particularly nasty graveyard desecration. The grave of a recently buried woman had been dug up. The coffin had been left stood on end and the corpse abandoned nearby.

What misery this must have caused relatives, for her to find no rest even in death. When I discussed this with Ramon, he was of the opinion vandals were to blame. I thought this was nonsense and told him why. Ordinary vandals don't have the patience nor the stamina to dig up a grave and remove a heavy coffin. They like their kicks instantly and with the minimum of effort; snapped car aerials, smashed up bus shelters and broken windows are their style. And this crime was premeditated. Spades, and tools to open the coffin must have been carried purposely to the graveyard. No, whoever carried this out were, in some way, connected with the occult.

In this book I have given various examples of individuals who have been prosecuted for murder and indecent assault, and have claimed to be witches, Satanists, or connected with the occult in some milder way. In most of the proven cases which spring to mind, the felon has been a loner. Like any other social activity, witchcraft is a gregarious occupation, in the sense thtat they form covens and temples. Yet, as Ramon said to me, anyone can buy three or four books on occultism and then call themselves a 'witch' or a 'Satanist'.

Witchcraft seems to attract four different types of people: Those genuinely searching for universal truth; those who see it as a road to power and the domination of others; those who want to be dominated; and the sensationalists.

The Occult Census carried out by Christopher Bray and his staff in 1989, revealed the fact that most occultists were between twenty and thirty nine years of age, with only 12% of respondents over fifty. Many were professional people and some quite wealthy. Only 10% were unemployed. Political alignment was primarily with the Green Party and the Liberal Democrats. Although 43% thought witchcraft could be used to bring about harm, only 14% admitted working black magic.

Psychopaths like Manson, David Berkowitz and Ramirez like it because of its dark mystery, because it deals in hidden things, and above all because the Church believes it is the reversal of all that is good and decent. Paedophiles see it as a means of impressing teenagers and children, and using it to drive fear into them as a way to guarantee silence.

As for future cases of alleged Satanic ritual abuse, objectivity is needed all round. Social workers need to note down statements without reinforcing 'abused' individuals through their own belief system. Likewise, police officers need to suspend disbelief and thoroughly check such allegations out. Of course the interests of the child should be paramount - something that has been sadly lacking in recent cases.

Witchcraft, as an alternative, but not competing, belief system to Christianity seems to be harmless to the person who has a healthy balanced mind. Like Christianity, witchcraft, or occultism, can be perverted by the hand of man. Power is a neutral force which can be bent to good or ill, like money. But is witchcraft intrinsically evil? I think the conclusion of an objective summing up, must be: case unproven... But that is not the same as saying 'no'.

SOURCES

Branston, Brian: *The Lost Gods Of England* (Thames & Hudson) 1974

Cavendish, Richard (Editor): *Man Myth & Magic* part-work (Purnell) 1971

Donovan, Frank: *Never On A Broomstick* (Allen & Unwin) 1973.

Farrar, Janet & Stuart: *The Life And Times Of A Modern Witch* (Piatkus) 1987

Farrar, Janet & Stuart: *The Witches' Goddess* (Hale) 1987

Gardner, G. B.: *The Meaning Of Witchcraft* (Aquarian Press) 1959

Gooch, Stan: *Creatures From Inner Space* (Rider) 1984

Hansen, Chadwick: *Witchcraft At Salem* (Arrow) 1988

Irvine, Doreen: *From Witchcraft To Christ* (Concordia) 1974

King, Francis X.: *Witchcraft And Demonology* (Hamlyn) 1987

Logan, Kevin: *Paganism And The Occult* (Kingsway) 1988

Owen, Gale R.: *Rites And Religions Of The Anglo-Saxons* (David & Charles) 1981

Peel, Edgar & Pat Southern: *The Trials Of The Lancashire Witches* (David & Charles) 1972

Randles, Jenny & Peter Hough: *Death By Supernatural Causes?* (Grafton) 1988

Shareth, Ramon: *Orthodox Satanism/Benelism* (Unpublished)

Smith, Michelle & Lawrence Pazder: *Michelle Remembers* (Michael Joseph) 1981

Terry, Maury: *The Ultimate Evil* (Grafton) 1989
Valiente, Doreen: *The Rebirth Of Witchcraft* (Hale) 1989
Wilson, Colin: *The Occult* (Mayflower) 1972
Raz Kathab Mashal Scriptures (Unpublished)
SHE (The National Magazine Company) Various issues
Various national and local newspapers named in text.
The Bible: Revised Standard Version

INDEX

194